BEYOND RESILIENT

Advance Praise

"Evidence-based, accessible, and eminently practical, this book provides the guidelines for ecstatic growth. In fact, reading *Beyond Resilient* is itself a growth experience."

—**Tal Ben-Shahar**, author of *Being Happy*

"Marc Cordon is the unapologetic coach. He not only offers you words for the molasses gap between your current self and your ideal self, he offers you a bridge for crossing it. Along this journey, you'll find Marc to be honest, funny, insightful, and strengths-based. Indeed, he is doing what the best coaches do—modeling one's best self through teaching."

—**Ryan M. Niemiec**, Psy.D., author of *Character Strengths Interventions: A Field Guide for Practitioners* and *Mindfulness and Character Strengths*; Education director and psychologist of the global nonprofit VIA Institute on Character

"*Beyond Resilient* is a must-read for life coaches at all levels who are ready to add financial success and fulfillment to their resume."

—**Bruce D. Schneider**, Founder, Institute for Professional Excellence in Coaching (iPEC) & author of *Uncovering the Life of Your Dreams*

"Marc Cordon is BEYOND BRILLIANT in this book! He boldly breaks the mold of what you might expect with refreshing and unique thoughts that are essential for any professional coach serious about taking business and life to a whole new level!"

—**Jeffrey St Laurent**, author of *Being Fulfilled* & Founder of SellingCoaching.com

"In his book *Beyond Resilient: A Coach's Guide to Ecstatic Growth*, Marc Cordon artfully weaves together inspiring stories with research-based methods to help professional coaches thrive in their work and lives. From the opening quote by Maslow ("What one can be, one must be.") to the final quote by Bruce Lee, I finished this book in one sitting. It is creative and humorous, edgy and relatable—a must-read if you are a professional coach. And it offers practices and wisdom for all who wish to live into their potential."

—**Jane Anderson**, facilitator, coach, & author of *30 Days of Character Strengths: A Guided Practice to Boost Your Relationships, Achievement and Well-Being*

"You can feel Cordon's energy and enthusiasm pumping you up with each turn of the page. His approach to playing the game of life rings true for my own coaching journey as I am sure it will for many others!"

—**Erin NeSmith** CPC, ELI-MP, Founder of Grow Into You Foundation

"A quick and powerful read! As a how-to guide, this book is brimming with straightforward, researched strategies anyone can use to overcome obstacles to creating a flourishing coaching business and a life that simply works."

—**Liz Fisch**, Senior Vice President, Institute for Professional Excellence in Coaching (iPEC)

"*Beyond Resilient* will take you and your coaching business to the next level. Marc Cordon weaves in his masterful positive psychology concepts into the book having the reader take advantage of his or her brain for immense growth. He helps us to move past our inner gremlins and focus on our strengths. Not only will this book propel you in your coaching business journey, it will help you in your personal life, begging you to ask the question, "what gets you out of bed in the morning?" Creating and having your dream business is on the other end of this book thanks to the living gamefully coach himself, Marc Cordon. I recommend this book, *Beyond Resilient*, and working with Marc if you want to awaken the unapologetic coach within you and receive his life-changing guidance. Initiate lasting change. Now."

—**Melissa Morrison**, author of *Unstick Your Stuck*

"Marc Cordon is the voice for coaches who want to steer their business to the top. As an emerging coach, I identify with the inner gremlins that many of us coaches encounter, since despite our servants' hearts, often, our inner gremlins block us from fulfilling our highest purpose to serve our clients. Whether you are a rebel, a maverick or an iconoclast, we have to be unapologetic, tenacious, respect the best interest of the people we're serving and most of all, LOVE our clients as the author has clearly outlined in this very significant book for coaches."

—**Belen "Belle" Grand** ARNP, MSN,
author of *Family Matters*

"Beyond Resilient will change lives. Readers will find power where they were once stopped. Marc Cordon's ability to deal with the tough issues in a connected way is art. My biggest takeaway from working with him is how authentic and elevating his energy is. I always grow from my interactions and have the experience of being a better man because of his gifts."

—**David Vletas**, entrepreneur & author of
Jumping Off the Edge Responsibly

"Marc's book is a breath of fresh air for coaches! He lays out how to coach as a calling and does it in an entertaining way (any book with Star Wars and pop culture references gets my vote). I highly recommend it!"

—**Marc Mawhinney**, coach, Natural Born Coaches

"Marc's authenticity is contagious and framework is rock solid. An equally enjoyable and useful read!"

—**Nicole Stottlemyer**, Founder of
Nicole Stottlemyer Coaching

"I have known Marc for many years as a colleague and a friend at Emory University. Then and as now in his book, Marc was always able to take the ideas from leading scholars and academic publications and make them both more accessible and practical in terms of how to use that science to change lives. Do you want a change in life? Then check out *Beyond Resilient* now."

—**Corey Keyes**, Professor of Sociology, Emory University & co-author of *Flourishing: Positive Psychology and the Life Well-Lived*

"Cordon crawls into the minds of anyone who feels a true calling to become a professional coach. He articulates obstacles for new coaches with full relatability and gusto, all while reminding us that big possibilities exist on the other side of our greatest risks and challenges."

—**Nina Cashman**, Founder & coach, Pave Your Way & Lead Trainer, Institute for Professional Excellence in Coaching

BEYOND
RESILIENT
The Coach's Guide
to Ecstatic Growth

Marc Cordon

NEW YORK

LONDON • NASHVILLE • MELBOURNE • VANCOUVER

BEYOND RESILIENT
The Coach's Guide to Ecstatic Growth

© 2019 **Marc Cordon**

Published in New York, New York, by Morgan James Publishing in partnership with Difference Press. Morgan James is a trademark of Morgan James, LLC. www.MorganJamesPublishing.com

The Morgan James Speakers Group can bring authors to your live event. For more information or to book an event visit The Morgan James Speakers Group at www.TheMorganJamesSpeakersGroup.com.

ISBN 978-1-64279-028-3 paperback
ISBN 978-1-64279-029-0 eBook
Library of Congress Control Number: 2018937611

Cover Design by:
Rachel Lopez
www.r2cdesign.com

Interior Design by:
Bonnie Bushman
The Whole Caboodle Graphic Design

In an effort to support local communities, raise awareness and funds, Morgan James Publishing donates a percentage of all book sales for the life of each book to Habitat for Humanity Peninsula and Greater Williamsburg.

Get involved today! Visit
www.MorganJamesBuilds.com

To Zac, Pax, Brady, Bryan & Melissa
May you never hesitate to set your towers ablaze

To Mom & Dad
May we never forget the towers you
left to make a better life for us

TABLE OF CONTENTS

INTRODUCTION

"What one can be, one must be."
—Abraham Maslow

So you didn't have 2.5 babies before you turned 30. Perhaps the promotion, for which you desperately postured yourself, came and went with no avail. Or maybe you miss being a hopeful daydreamer with a pocketful of aspirations. Do you wish you could go back to a time when you had less debt and backaches and start your coaching business knowing what you know now? Standing at a crossroads, you now reflect from where you came and toward where you want to go with nervous anticipation.

Don't look now, but here comes your man Maslow with this deceptively powerful quote: *What one can be, one must be.* This rings true to any human on an epic journey and is exponentially visceral to an aspiring coach like you. From my experience, you are not only reading this book because you are on the journey to becoming what you *must be*, but because you've been called to be a life-Sherpa for others as they scale their personal mountains and reach new levels of actualization and self-transcendence.

The difference between *your current place in the universe* and *your infinite potential* can be fully motivating and inspiring. You see a vision where all domains of your life— work, love, play— are simultaneously firing at full capacity. You want to optimize your time, focus, and productivity, and ready yourself for a life more fulfilling. Yet the gap between your *current self* and your *ideal self* can also trigger anxiety, doubt, and even shame because you haven't reached your full potential by now.

Like A Rubber Band

Experience the discomfort of the gap between your *current self* and your *ideal self* like that of a rubber band being stretched. As you become increasingly aware of the distance between your current and ideal self, you are pulling the rubber band. The larger the gap, the more tension you feel. If you rate high on the flinch-factor scale, you might even be showing an anticipatory wince just in case of a massive rubber band pop.

That tension you feel may be coming from the fact that people depend on you at work or home. So to pursue a vision of serving more people and having more freedom might be a concept that jeopardizes their trust that you can be their go-to person. Maybe you had an epiphany asking yourself, "There's got to be more to life than this?" And the resulting tension came from the realization that you will need to go against the status quo to become your ideal self.

Perhaps your younger self used to dream of serving a movement that makes an epic impact on the world, and again you thought you'd have that all accomplished by the time you turned some arbitrary age. So the tension would come from holding onto your dream, but feeling a sense of urgency that you need to make things happen very quickly.

How does this appear in your daily life? At work, you may feel like you've outgrown your dream job. Now you're just going through the motions of a rat race and figuring out how to make coaching sustainable without looking like a fool as you transition. You wake up exhausted, wondering how your once dream job became an object of despise. At home, especially if you are the main emotional or financial support of the family, you feel lonely. You don't want to let anyone down. Amongst your peers, you put on a mask that everything is hunky-dory because that's all they've known of you. They can't hear that your inner dialogue has been changing lately. You get upset when you see people half as smart as you, who work half as hard, following their dreams and subsequently crushing it. At the end of the day, when you remove all of your masks, you jump into the shower and get so caught up in your inner world that you don't even notice when the water has gone ice cold.

You lie in bed thinking about your past, your future, what has happened and what hasn't happened in your life. You hop out of bed and read one of Oprah's manifestation books of the week, and ask yourself, "Why do they make this sound so easy?"

The Curse and Blessing of Tension

Your awareness of the need to become a coach is a curse. There is no real pathway to become one, but become one you must as you don't know how much longer you can live in this silent distress. You don't want to make a wrong move, but other coaches have taken a million routes to start their coaching businesses. This is also a blessing on the grandest of scales. Because to design your path, one not bound to blueprints constructed by a status quo, means that you can see the invisible tapestry that keeps many people living quietly, desperately fulfilling other people's dreams. The tension you currently feel is the same one that is calling you to take the first step on your journey to become a *bad mama jama* (if you're a Jen Sincero fan), live with arête (if you're down with the Greeks), or transform into your ideal self if Maslow's your man.

Who This Book Is For

Over the course of 15 years, I have coached, advised, and wrestled with this tension. This topic has come up more often than I can count. This book is for anyone experiencing this existential pull, but more specifically, it is for the aspiring coach who is ready to create a life truer to their goals. You will need to dig deep to bury the aspiring coach and fully inspirit the unapologetic one. Choosing this book means you probably already have your shovel ready. Let's put it to work.

Chapter One

WHEN QUIET DESPERATION IGNITES A FIRE

"The mass of men lead lives of quiet desperation. What is called resignation is confirmed desperation. From the desperate city, you go into the desperate country and have to console yourself with the bravery of minks and muskrats. A stereotyped but unconscious despair is concealed even under what are called the games and amusements of mankind. There is no play in them, for this comes after work. But it is a characteristic of wisdom not to do desperate things."
—Henry David Thoreau

I f you are reading this book, you've already realized that you do not want to lead a life of quiet desperation. Somewhere along your coach training you've had an "AHA!" moment that is making it very difficult to go back to a job you once loved but now almost loathe. Yet to live that actualized life where you create space for transformation upon transformation feels like you're standing on the edge of two tall towers. The tower ahead of you holds all your dreams as a coach. The tower upon which you stand represents your current life. This tower is so old that it is virtually condemned.

You've been able to deal with the creature comforts of your old tower until now because here comes Maslow's tension again. You see the face of your vision of coaching right in front of you and know that you can no longer stay in your current situation. So with that insight, don't look down, your building has been set on fire.

When you realized that you were putting in too much work and burning out over outcomes that you were no longer passionate about, your fire was lit.

When you said to yourself, "I want to be happier," your fire was lit.

When you declared that you want the courage to live a more authentic life, not the life others expect of you, your fire was lit.

When you wanted to spend more time with friends and family, your fire was lit.

And when you committed to using your courage to express yourself, your fire was lit (Ware, 2011).

You set the right thing ablaze: your current life. A life where you have outgrown the challenges of your current work, to the point where you may feel as if you are just going through the motions. A life where you don't like admitting that you're looking at other people's entrepreneurial accomplishments and feeling jealousy or envy. A life where you've made a good name for yourself, where your family depends on you, and where you have a good reputation with your community.

It may be scary now, but trust me, it gets better. When the time comes, you'll unfurl your wings and land safely atop your dream coaching business. Even if your family, friends, and colleagues don't understand it now, when the time is right, they will see you perched on your new tower and say that you deserve to be there. They'll come around. Just continue to live gamefully.

If you're finishing a coach training program, you are in a perfect place to become one. But you have a decision to make, "Is coaching the solution to your quiet desperation?" If it's not, you may find yourself perched upon a burning coaching tower in a few years.

If it is, I'm here to be a part of what could arguably be the toughest part of the coaching journey: your emergence as an *unapologetic coach*— one who serves boldly and will never be ashamed again of who they are. This journey goes beyond resilience. It serves as the activation energy to ecstatic growth despite personal anarchy.

I Just Want Relief!

I screamed that at the top of my lungs in front of my iPEC (Institute for Professional Excellence in Coaching) cohort of coach trainees in October 2016. I played the role of a client in a fishbowl activity with our coach facilitator, Kyle, modeling the coaching process. And when Kyle probed deeper as to my goals in the next year, I couldn't take it anymore. I didn't know how much money I wanted to make. I didn't know what my coaching niche would be. I just knew I wanted relief!

I knew there was something more for me than what I was currently doing. I thought I was losing my mind to question the stability and the name prestige that I had built up. I was a college administrator and in a Ph.D. program for College Student Affairs Administration. Though I always had a passion for the human development aspect of things, I could care less about naming programs or conduct codes or meetings that felt more like ego-driven urinating contests. I fell in love with positive psychology and saw its application to human development in my life and the people's lives around me.

It's an understatement to say how good the University was to me as a student and as a professional. For over 13 years, I was given space to create identity development retreats, sit on the University senate and score some sweet grants. I was handed opportunity upon opportunity to guest lecture in classes, spearhead summer internships, and even create a mini-course on happiness that was in line with the vision of many to turn it into a credit-bearing, revenue-generating academic minor or track. I was receiving offers to work with even more prestigious schools with bigger budgets, was mentioned in a national college health conference for having an innovative practice to tell student stories through assessment, and even hustled to get flourishing on our department-wide strategic plan.

Even with all the apparent accolades, it wasn't enough. My appetite could not be satiated. And I distinctly remember three "AHA!" moments that shifted my whole being.

First, I remember a lecture in which Dr. Paul Bloom from Yale discussed the notion of the *hedonic treadmill*. He described it as the idea that we continuously habituate to short-term happiness. So, for example, if I won an award, I'd feel good at the moment, but a year later, I'd want another one to boost me back up. And the more and more you stay on this treadmill, the faster the speed and the higher the incline. You work hard. Your happiness is ephemeral. In the long-term, the most you may have acquired is regrets. What a nihilistic view of happiness!

I was disturbed by the number of years I was on that treadmill, almost as far back as I could remember, and tantamount, I was concerned by the nagging feeling that I was indoctrinating college students to stay on their treadmills. What's worse? I didn't know how to step off the treadmill even though I knew that I was on a path of temporary short-term highs that were getting me nowhere. The higher in the organization I went, the more administrative malarkey that didn't resonate with me. If I chose to go the academic route, I saw the same treadmill— from researcher to assistant to associate to tenure to what? Department head or administrator that goes to more meaningless meetings? But how could I turn back after over 13 years?

My second "AHA!" moment happened while listening to my colleague, Dr. Corey Keyes, describe the notion of human flourishing as feeling good and functioning well. If you just feel good, with no purpose, then you are *settling*. Like the hedonic treadmill, I felt like I had so much more to give the world, but was so wrought with the fear of making the leap of faith that I settled for the quick-acting, but not lasting, happiness. On the other end, to function well with purpose and meaning, without experiencing that daily, quick-acting happiness, is called *striving*. To act on your purpose and not be on the treadmill is amazing, but to not get regular happiness from it, to strive, puts you on the road to distress and burnout. When I heard Corey describe flourishing in that way, I realized that I was *striving* in my Ph.D. program, *settling* at work, and flourishing absolutely nowhere.

The final "AHA!" moment occurred while giving a lecture to alumni and students about happiness and how all of the aforementioned concepts were coming together. I discussed the hedonic treadmill and Keyes' ideas of striving, settling, and flourishing and told remarkable stories of overcoming them, but what I realized in the middle of the lecture, was that this once very fresh lecture had become stale and was now over two years old. Two years, and I didn't have a single new slide about my life to tell. It became painfully obvious that I was going to need to face the fact the happiness guy needed to now deal with his own happiness or lack thereof. It was time to boogie or get off the pot when it came to my growth.

When you're grass-fed daily, low-potency doses of messages that make you feel helpless, invisible, or "less-than" what you know you must be, you might react in several ways— feeling like the universe is conspiring against you or what appears to be a random volcanic explosion. I had the latter when Coach Kyle dug deep in our iPEC fishbowl session. I knew that I was settling and striving for mediocrity. I wanted to spend more time with my family. I served my job well and outgrew it.

We're All Hermit Crabs

At some point, you outgrew your shell. What was once a perfect fit had become constricting. I needed to get out. I needed to find a bigger space but knew that moving from one shell to the other was what I feared the most. I needed relief. And after that, although it was scary, I'd find myself a new home with room to grow.

And with that, I declared that I didn't want to attend meetings for meetings' sake. I didn't want to hand out water or condoms when *Smashmouth* was playing at our school's homecoming. I wanted to work with more people as they found their purpose. I wanted to do what I was already doing, but more streamlined and on a bigger scale.

Be careful about what you wish. Because when you throw out a life change and let it soak down to your DNA, your mind, body, and soul go on a seek-and-destroy mission. Consciously or not, after I made my declaration at iPEC, I started taking action toward the "relief" I so desperately screamed for. I always ignored my health with work because I was so stuck on the treadmill. But after I announced to my iPEC group that I wanted off, my body got violently sick at the thought of going back to work.

And by the end of that October, the University terminated their contract with me. While the first 12 hours elicited a range of emotions, my iPEC declaration became true. Whether I liked it or not, relief was here.

My time at the University could have come to a more fitting ending to what I wished. I was pushed out of the nest and needed to figure out if the wings that I thought I had were real.

I don't believe in coincidences. Yet the manuscript for this book is due precisely one year to the day that I asked for relief to live a dream life. It makes me grin that again I want relief in the form of finishing this manuscript. This time, I don't feel victimized or angry. I'm choosing to push myself— and loving every millisecond of it.

With no backup job, a few clients, and a web domain, I took every positive psychology concept and put it to practice. In turn, I had the privilege of experiencing the ups, downs, and all-arounds of establishing a business very quickly and doing what I absolutely love doing the most— empowering as many people as possible while having as much fun as possible. In October 2016, my tribes fed me in many forms— from new clients, to my certifications in positive psychology from the Wholebeing Institute, and coaching through iPEC. Now it's time for me to feed you. This book is a distillation of everything I learned in one year of disciplined practice.

Are you settling, striving, and ready to answer your call to serve the greater good? Good. It's playtime.

Chapter Two
A FRAMEWORK TO LIVE GAMEFULLY

"Empty your mind. Be formless, shapeless like water."
—Bruce Lee

T he world sends us messages of what's in, what's out, best practices, guidelines, timelines, deadlines. Here's a lifeline. Becoming a skeptic of these messages and constructs is inherently a good thing. Yet it feels like a personal anarchy is taking place within you. It's disrupting enough to unground you and send you into a dizzying existential spin. You're freeing your mind of human constructs and getting a small glimpse of both the simplicity and expansiveness of natural law. Your inner revolution is just the uprising you need to create space and clarity to see your next step, and an immense move at that.

I offer you a framework that is light and almost invisible, but present in everything that grows. It is meant to have massive space for your creativity, tenacity, and improvisation to flourish. It is a framework for a gameful life. It contains four principles—objectives, obstacles, feedback loops, and choice (McGonigal, 2011). Together they comprise four pinholes connected by the thinnest thread made of the most robust graphene.

Gameful Principle #1: Objective

This may be the most crucial question in the book. Don't skip it.

On your worst day, what gets you out of bed?

It is easy to answer when you have momentum, just as it is easy to sail when the wind is brisk. But try answering this question when you are in the middle of a doldrum ... in a sea where there is no discernible movement ... with no land in the visible horizon to give you directionality.

This question alludes to the first foundational principle of living gamefully. To have a singular objective in which to turn at your worst moment gives you a purpose. It doesn't have to be your quintessential life purpose, just *a* purpose. Even if you respond in the most snarky ways like, "I answered this question to get to the next chapter" or "Because I have to," you're playing the game well. Snark is cool with me since I know that I'm asking a frustrated coach to write down their goal. Just don't forget when someone offers you a warm meal, you best clean your plate, *hungry Jack*. So if you said something like, "It's my objective to have an objective," that works too.

Write it on a post-it note and keep it with you. Save it on your phone. Answer the question as best as you can and know that you have a reason to engage with the world.

Gameful Principle #2: Rules

In games, rules are external confines that restrict play. They create unnecessary obstacles.

We live in a society of constructed unnecessary obstacles. If you are working for a company, you have a deadline. It fixes the time limit for you to achieve a goal and, thus, challenges your performance.

Most of the time, we're learning the rules as we go. We're figuring what we can and can't accomplish given expanding or contracting confines. If you ever saw the short-lived, but oh-so-amazing television show *The Greatest American Hero*, you might relate to the main character's trial and error of figuring out rules. Essentially, aliens task a mild-mannered substitute teacher to save the world and bestow upon him a suit that gives him superhuman qualities. Here's the rub, the teacher loses the instruction manual. So the game for the substitute teacher is to save the world while figuring out the rules, the true extent of his insane powers. How art imitates life.

Gaming Principle #3: Feedback

Even if your goal is a little wobbly and hard to articulate and you are not exactly sure of the rules, pay attention to when you feel energized and when you feel drained.

Simply being aware of feeling energized or enervated is the beginning of exploring the nature of "cause and effect" in your routines, roles, and people around you. Games have feedback loops systematically embedded into them. Without receiving feedback, we wouldn't know our progress toward our goal achievement. In many sports, it's measured in points. It's even in simple board games. For example, in the game Operation, you must successfully remove the Cavity Sam's bones without touching your "surgical" tweezers to the edges. If you are unsuccessful, the game lets you know through an annoying buzz and the lighting up of the patient's nose. If you are successful, you get paid depending on the difficulty of the procedure.

We have these feedback loops built into our everyday life. These feedback loops are individualized. And identifying them can be a game in itself.

Let's identify your first feedback loop. Make two lists— one answering what energizes you and the other explaining what exhausts you. Make them exhaustive lists by thinking about people, places, roles, responsibilities, tasks, etc. And circle the top three most impactful influencers on each list.

Congratulations, you have your first feedback loop on playing the game.

Gaming Principle #4: Choice

The cool thing about where you are at in life is that you have some form of choice in what you engage and disengage. Even in the most oppressive environments, you can still find a freedom of choice. Your freedom to choose has a significant impact on motivation, which leads to the completion of your goals.

So here's the first game if you're up for it.

How long can you inhale before you can't take any more air in?

- What is the objective?
- What is the rule?
- What is the feedback loop?
- Is it voluntary?

If you can control your inhale, you can become a successful coach.

What's in the box?! Within each chapter, I'll present micro-content, for example, "tiny little classes," for your consideration. The tiny little classes span across the chapters outlined below. If this is your first read, progress through each class in sequence. Breathe in all of it. Exhale what you don't need.

Within this framework, an empty canvas, a hot mic, and a blank page await. This is the space for you to have a blast creating your dream business and protect you from the stabbing criticism of others. Before you enter, I am pleased to share a few gifts— a brush and watercolors, a glass of water to clear your throat, and a quill and inkwell. These are the elements presented in the next few chapters.

- Magnify Your Strengths (Chapter Three)
- Overcome Your Inner Gremlins (Chapter Four)
- Excite Your Tribe (Chapter Five)
- Initiate Lasting Change (Chapter Six)
- Evolve an Antifragile Mindset (Chapter Seven)

These five elements will help you build universes inside of the most straightforward framework. It is the art of living gamefully. I'm 100 percent sure you can alleviate the tension between your *current self* and your *ideal self.* This book will do this … and more. I only ask that you apply these concepts. Practice is the only way to make the tension go away. Reading about transformation without praxis is about as useful as learning about sex and not having it. It's just a little bit different— or so I'm told.

Press start to begin.

Chapter Three
MAGNIFY YOUR SIGNATURE STRENGTHS

"Success is achieved by development of our strengths, not by elimination of our weakness."
—Marilyn Vos Savant

E veryone is born with variations that make them slightly different from the norm. We have been raised to be prototypical workers, lovers, and players— ones that do not deviate from external standards. A prototype is an amalgam of averages— average number of kids, average income, average number of cars. These become archetypical molds for our psyche but have the potential to spit out mindless automatons that live in quiet desperation.

Your ideal self is nowhere close to the average. Your ideal self is an outlier living in the farthest outreach beyond your imagination. So while your variations may be perceived as freakish mutations to the norm, they are your signature strengths. When fully utilized, they create more fulfillment as you dare to move to the outskirts of the norm and become who you've wanted to be as a coach.

Imagine you were born with wings. At a young age, you made social comparisons and noticed others did not have wings— other kids, your mentors, even people in the media. So you hid them. All the while your wings have remained your dormant strength. We live in a society where we improve our deficiencies in the hopes of becoming some unrealistic human paradigm. Paradigm of what? Don't ignore your flaws, but don't hide your strengths either.

Class 1: Finding Your Best Self Using Extrinsic & Intrinsic Strengths

"The idea of recognizing your strengths and using them in as versatile a way as you can is cool to me."
—Frank Ocean

To find your best self, look at what you perform well at and what brings you energy. Strengths come in two types, and it would be beneficial for you and your clients to differentiate the two for deeper self-understanding.

Production and output measure the first type of strength. If coaching is a strength, you see it as an external strength through scores on your oral exams, client referrals, and testimonials.

The second type of strength is measured by what fuels your strength.

While studying with the Wholebeing Institute, I picked up a simple exercise that helps you distinguish the two different strengths and helps identify your ideal self.

Part 1— Identify Your Extrinsic Strengths

Take 20 minutes to write about your strengths— the things that you are good at. Be as specific as you can and give examples of situations in which you expressed your strengths. There are no right answers to this question. Without much concern for grammar or clarity, write down whatever comes to mind.

Part 2— Identify Your Intrinsic Strengths

Take 20 minutes to write about those things that give you strength, those things that energize you. Be as specific as you can and provide examples of situations in which you expressed your strengths. There are no right answers to this question. Without much concern for grammar or clarity, write down whatever comes to mind.

Part 3— Find Your Best Self

Circle the things that appeared in both your intrinsic and extrinsic strengths. These are aspects of your best self.

Use this to assist your clients.

For yourself as a coach, look at your best self. What elements of coaching are parts of your best self? Perhaps there's a specific population you like working with or a particular type of life opportunity by which you are well versed and energized. Do these align with your niche and purpose?

Class 2: Know, Use, & Align Your Signature Strengths

"Confidence is a much more complex phenomenon that comes from experiencing one's strengths in action."
—Rosabeth Moss Canter

The VIA Institute of Character has conducted several strength studies and cited that knowing, using, and aligning your strengths with different parts of your life show increases in happiness, engagement, meaning, viewing work-as-a-calling, productivity, relationship satisfaction, vitality/passion, and coping.

Identify Your Signature Strengths

Signature strengths are those strengths that are most central to you and are most energizing when used. Take the VIA Character Survey for free on http://marccordon.pro.viasurvey.org to get your personalized report on all 24 of your strengths. Your top five to seven strengths are your signature strengths. Keep your printout close, as you'll be using it for more reflections in this chapter.

Knowing Vs. *Using* Your Signature Strengths

Does it seem like you are using your signature strengths regularly? How can you employ them in your coaching business?

Individuals who know their signature strengths are nine times more likely to be flourishing compared to those who do not. Those who are regularly using their signature strengths are 18 times more likely to be flourishing compared to those who do not.

Strengths Alignment

Aligning your signature strengths with your work creates opportunities for more engagement and productivity. If you are passionate about your job, it will bolster your job as a meaningful vocation.

- Identify your top five most frequent work tasks or responsibilities.
- Choose your top signature strength, and write down how you will use it in alignment with your work tasks for the next five days.
- After this workweek is over, choose the next signature strength, and repeat.

Continue this until you've used all of your signature strengths (Niemiec, 2017).

Class 3: Spot Strengths as Often As Possible

"If you want to view paradise, simply look around and view it."

—Gene Wilder

Nothing may be more delightful than seeing that mad scientist Wonka singing these lines in *Pure Imagination*. Wilder humanizes the chocolatier making him a generous, a genius creator, and a hopeful optimist in an otherwise dreary world. Isn't that what you are trying to do as an entrepreneur? Spotting strengths creates opportunities where other people see desolation and despair. So if the candy man can, you can.

As you get the hang of all 24 character strengths from the VIA Character Survey, build your awareness through observation from a strengths perspective.

In a coaching situation, using *strength spotting* with your client by telling them the advantage you observe. This is powerful on multiple levels. First, your client will understand themselves a little deeper. Second, it shows that you're listening thoroughly and intensely.

For example, you might say, "To be working with this gremlin holding you back from starting a coaching business over these weeks, and to see you just go for it, I completely commend your bravery. It gives me, even more, confidence that you're ready for the next challenge."

In any aspect of your personal life, explain *strength spotting* to your partner and ask them to observe you as you exhibit your strengths. You may be very surprised just how many strengths you incorporate in your daily life.

It may feel a little…well…wonky at first. Because people aren't primed to respond to compliments. Once they trust that there's *no catch*, that you aren't spitting backhanded compliments, *strength spotting* will empower them for greatness. Remember, just knowing your strengths and how you use them, not only makes you more efficient in your tasks, but much happier. Tuning your perspective to strength spotting can make a huge difference. "Want to change the world? There's nothing to it."

—**Gene Wilder**

Class 4: Use Your Strength in a New Way

"Innovation is taking two things that already exist and putting them together in a new way."

—**Tom Freston**

My client May was an outstanding volunteer coordinator in hospice care for many years. In addition to recruiting, she managed to retain ridiculous numbers of volunteers. When I started coaching May, she was launching her life-coaching business on a full-time basis. She didn't have very many leads. She was questioning whether she could generate new clients.

When asked what she wanted to do in the first session, May wanted to talk about how she could convert new clients.

I asked, "When you were conducting your volunteer recruitment and intake interviews, what qualities did you effectively use that contributed to such high recruitment and retention rates?"

May was quick to reply, "There was definitely a lot of empathy, listening for what the volunteer wanted, follow up to see if there were any questions I could answer. I gave clear expectations of their volunteer work, and also talked about how transformative this experience would be for them."

"How do you think those strengths from recruiting in hospice care would translate into talking to a potential client about having a transformative experience with you?"

May thought they would transfer well. And her next steps were to develop a lead conversion script that used her strengths that were already apparent from her last career in a new way.

Numerous studies show that using your strength in a new way both elevates happiness and decreases depression.

You have multiple decades of wisdom from your past experiences. Reinventing yourself has nothing to do with erasing those experiences and everything to do with pivoting on them. These are the soft skills that aren't taught in textbooks but make all the difference when you interact with humans. For your coaching business, what strengths have you successfully used in the past, and how can you use them in your coaching venture (Niemiec, 2017)?

Class 5: Use the Superpower of Self-distancing

"There is a God part in you. The consciousness. The pure Self. Learn to listen to the voice of that Power."
—Amit Ray

Have you ever seen the WWJD bracelets? They stand for "What Would Jesus Do?" The bracelets serve as reminders of living a virtuous Christian life. Jesus was kind of a rebel and hot head, like many of my ideal clients, so I'm totally down with that. Though I'm pretty sure the Church's marketing team did not intend for kids to slap on a few of these bands and start throwing around tables in their local temple.

But let's say you're not feeling the bracelet. Let's etch the letter *Y* over the *J*. And there you have it: *What Would You Do?* This is no longer a hidden camera show hosted by John Quinones, but a way of constructing your ideal self.

In the coaching world, it's pretty fashionable for coaches to name their programs things like *Unleashing Your Inner Superpowers*. This is one of the ways to do it.

Jane McGonigal (2016) describes this technique as self-distancing. In it, you imagine all the strengths of your ideal self, even give your ideal self a nickname. Mine is Manila Ice, and he's one *bad dude*.

Use self-distancing when applying your strengths in especially challenging situations. There tends to be a lag between thinking, overthinking, and acting. You can sometimes get caught in the overthinking part, which results in no action. Social distancing decreases the lag, as the challenges are happening to someone else and not you. So instead of visualizing what I would do in certain situations, I imagine Manila Ice saving the day.

I've used this with several athletes who want mindset coaching in team sports. In the coaching world, I use this with clients hesitant to make a decision. This depends on the client. This technique worked particularly well with my client Caroline, who would initially hesitate to respond to her dream client, because she didn't want to lose the client.

Depending on the context, self-distancing has several benefits. In the past, it reduces stress and anxiety. In the present, willpower. In the future, it helps with viewing things as a gameful challenge rather than a threat. On a mindful level, to distance yourself expands consciousness. You move away from self-consciousness and toward god-consciousness. To live in a consciousness larger than yourself is to make yourself open to more moments of synchronicity and awe.

Chapter Four
OVERCOME YOUR INNER GREMLIN

"Real difficulties can be overcome; it is only the imaginary ones that are unconquerable."
—Theodore N. Vail

Gremlins represent the nagging inner voice that tells you that you're not good enough, qualified enough, or experienced enough to succeed as a coach or anything else. They heckle you mercilessly. They cause your esteem to take a nosedive and create havoc on your clarity to make decisions. They fortify beliefs with walls so thick that they limit your perception of opportunities. If you already magnified your signature strengths, gremlins construct illusionary ceilings— a deception to prevent you from flying.

In the art of living gamefully, overcoming your gremlins removes mental obstacles. These are imaginary rules that you impose on yourself.

Gremlins are immune to positive affirmations. They don't come in handy! Gremlins will quickly stomp on your attempt to counter-punch with inner dialogue. They feed on euphemisms like, "I'm good enough, smart enough, and doggonit people like me," the second you fall short. If you're passing this archaic weak sauce on to your clients, stop.

Even if you get to the point of a small win, gremlins create such doubt that you don't deserve the success that imposter syndrome can set it. Let's turn down the volume on the inner chatter so limiting beliefs or illusionary ceilings won't distract you.

Before proceeding, know that gremlins originate from your past. For example, someone's perfectionistic gremlin may originate from never feeling like their hard work was ever good enough for someone else's standards. As one of my mentors once told me, if you come to a locked fence that hinders your progress, a coach helps you figure out how to get to the other side, while a therapist helps you understand why the fence is locked. Gremlins are not only annoying, but they can potentially cause depression and anxiety. As you proceed to serve others, allow your coaches to coach, your healers to heal.

Note: This chapter contains my interpretation of the copyrighted work of Bruce D Schneider and the Institute for Professional Excellence in Coaching (iPEC).

Class 6: Self-Distance from Your Gremlin

"Just the two of us."
—Marshall Mathers

You are not your thoughts. Your inner dialogue, your chatter, your gremlin— you *hear* it, but it's not who you are. To look at it from a neurobiological standpoint, they originate from such a primitive part of the brain that it's often referred to as the reptilian brain. This is why I love the term "gremlin," because these psychological things seem very reminiscent of the lizard-like creatures who caused chaos when you fed Gizmo after midnight. This part of the brain is wired to keep us safe, sound, and out of danger. While necessary, the reptilian part of our brain becomes problematic when it takes over the cognitive and rational components. So you're not a loser, you just hear your old lizard brain yapping. Those thoughts become our beliefs. We believe that we're not worthy of being loved or succeeding as a coach. Eventually, our behaviors follow. I can't tell you the number of times that someone has said to me that they are their own biggest obstacle.

The self-distancing technique is incredibly helpful here.

- Name your gremlin. Any name— just not yours or a specific name that will attribute the gremlin to someone else.
- Imagine what your gremlin looks like. Or better yet, make a physical representation of your gremlin— a drawing, collage, be super creative.
- What is the gremlin saying to you?
- Feel free to make a few more if you distinguish between gremlins.

Here's the game: When you hear the gremlin talking to you, choose whether or not you want to believe what it's telling you.

One of the most fun and most powerful sessions that I had was with my client Matt who had created his ideal self-avatar and his gremlin. It already had this fight feel as Matt talked about his gremlin versus his ideal self. So we made it one. Knowing Matt was a huge wrestling fan, we set up the main event of *Wrestlemania* to be his gremlin versus his ideal self. I told him that the gremlin is the current world champion and you, as the previous, want it back. I pretended to be the announcer Mean Gene and Matt proceeded to deliver pipe bomb after pipe bomb on his gremlin. It was hellacious, but at the same time, it got really deep really quick. Matt talked about being "sick and tired of playing small ball" because he listened to this gremlin.

"There are no mistakes," he said. "And my whole life, you've made me second guess every move I've made! This stops tonight."

I stopped smiling. Ric Flair couldn't have said it any better.

It's incredible just how powerful you are when you don't overthink, have a champion's mindset, and are given an imaginary microphone.

I know you're reading this, Matt. Congratulations on earning your championship life after claiming it that night.

Class 7: Other People's Gremlins

"You aren't defined by the insecurities of others."
—Meghan Ann Hargis

The ecosystem composed of your family— immediate and extended— is dynamic. Changes sometimes come at a glacial pace, but very quick disrupters are always a possibility. A new addition to the family, moving, divorce— these are all disruptors that bring about rapid changes in homeostasis to the ecosystem. Members adopt new roles as new parents or become caretakers. They take on financial responsibilities when another loses a job. Announcing your intent to become an entrepreneur coach is a declaration of disruption. While a disruption is neither good nor bad, it can easily be interpreted as one or the other.

Our most virtuous loved ones can have mixed reactions to your declaration for several reasons. First, they don't want to see you fail, especially on a public scale. Second, if they depend on you, especially financially, they might be in direct opposition to your dream as it elicits the fear of losing stability within the ecosystem.

Everyone has gremlins, and these are just manifestations of gremlins inside of the people who love you. Their gremlins (and yours) will continue to make appearances during the most critical parts of your journey to become an unapologetic coach. Their appearances are good because change is afoot.

Don't allow these gremlins to build a wall around your dream. Your current building is afire, and you still know what's behind the wall. The tension will not go away.

Intuitively listen to what your family's and your friends' gremlins are trying to tell you. And be prepared to make a decision. Because sometimes the only way to tame the gremlin of your most virtuous friend— is to prove it wrong.

If you ever find yourself on the other end of someone's declaration, feel a loss of control, and allow your gremlin to speak its fears, ask yourself this:

What will continuing this behavior lead to two years from now?

If it's not an outcome you want, change your behavior now (Robbins, 2017).

Class 8: Taming Your Gremlin

"Just the two of us."
—Will Smith

The reptilian brain is also responsible for keeping you safe and sound by controlling your fight, flight or freeze response. So when this part of the brain takes precedence over our evolutionarily newer cognitive and rational ones, not only do we experience gremlins but we experience fight or flight reactions when there are no predators or dangers. Luckily, Herb Benson and William Proctor (2011) have conducted extensive research on this and have a way to counteract these inappropriate fight or flight responses and tame your gremlin's chatter.

The Relaxation Response

The relaxation response is simple to start and takes practice to master. Remember the challenge to control your breath in Chapter Two? Let's build on that.

- Inhale deeply (breathe so your stomach is going up and down and not your shoulders) but gently for about five seconds.
- Hold your breath for three seconds.
- Exhale for five seconds.
- Hold your breath for three seconds and repeat.
- Repeat for 12-15 minutes.
- As thoughts emerge, you know it's the reptilian brain still working. So just say, "Oh well."

The time differs per person, but you will feel the relaxation response kick in hard after a few minutes. It feels different depending on the individual. But most of my clients describe a heaviness, looseness or unwinding. I didn't know what to look for at first, but after a few days I could immediately feel mental stillness and it felt as if I had a great massage. Multiple repeated studies have shown that this technique not only calms chatter, but also has miraculous effects of some prescription drugs. But as you start to treat it as a game, your relaxation response and willpower fight your whacky reptilian fight, flight or freeze response.

Control your inhale to keep at bay the internal gremlins that are holding you back from becoming a coach. If you're in bed and the gremlin chatter becomes a nuisance, invoke the relaxation response. If you can control your breath, you can coach.

Class 9: Beat The Rush

*"I have a hard time finding the balance not beating myself
up when it doesn't happen as fast as I'd like it to, and not
wasting my time while I wait for it to happen."*
—Lin-Manuel Miranda

Your gremlin has a powerful weapon. At the first sign of perceived
danger or fear, the brain releases massive doses of cortisol. The
effect, called the spotlight effect, is an increased self-perception
of insecurity and self-doubt. Like inching to the edge of a cliff,
you will naturally want to retreat to safer ground. Again, when
it comes to your business, the reptilian brain does not know if
you are standing at a real precipice or a metaphorical one. But
in your coaching business, safer ground is a place where your
internal tension is the most stretched.

As an emerging coach, you'll feel this paralysis kick in when
you don't have sales experience and hesitate to call a lead. It's the
imposter feeling you get when charging a premium when you
are not master certified. It's running from opportunity when
you don't consider yourself a public speaker and have been
asked to keynote a positive psychology conference.

While you want to be critical during the creative process—
it's the only way new ideas are born— you don't want to let this
take over your business operations.

At the first sense of "real" or "fake" danger, cortisol is released within five seconds. An effective counterpunch is to count backward from five and take decisive action.

Your gremlin mind has automated so many processes of which are unaware that you can reprogram its feedback loop. If you are hesitating on any task in your business, do the following:

- Be aware of what you want to change (e.g. I want to have a sales call with a lead).
- Observe the automation (e.g. I feel tremendous self-doubt and prioritize another task).
- Count backward from five and act on what you want to change.

Like the Herb Benson technique, this allows your prefrontal (cognitive) brain to take charge and make more rational decisions (Robbins, 2017).

Class 10: Understand & Repurpose Your Gremlin

"The one to whom nothing was refused, whose tears were always wiped away by an anxious mother, will not abide being offended."

—De Ira

In the sport of roller derby, a "whip" is a maneuver in which a skater engages with her scoring teammate (the jammer). The result is a transfer of energy to the jammer that creates an incredibly fast rate of acceleration. When you repurpose your gremlin, it moves from being an antagonist to a teammate that can provide you the boost you need to reach unfounded rates of personal growth and prosperity. It's time to put roller skates on your gremlin!

Many of my clients enjoy being in an adversarial state with their gremlin and others have a more pacifist approach and want to make their gremlins an ally in their journey. If you were curious as to why you would make something that's been holding you back for so long an ally, it's because the reptilian brain has kept us as a species alive while we were running from animals that were higher on the food chain than us.

This is why the reptilian brain is not a bad thing. It just hasn't adapted as fast as we have evolved. So sometimes it will send us antiquated signals when there is no real threat of danger. It's why our heart starts rapidly thumping out of our chests and we flinch during a scary movie when the reality is we're sitting in a dark room watching projections on a wall. Didn't Plato warn us about this on a philosophical level in the *Analogy of the Cave*?

So one part of our brain is always trying to keep us safe and sound. But if these thoughts are not our own, what are gremlins but the earliest versions of overprotective helicopter parents. They hover over us and micromanage our every move. They tell us not to be a coach entrepreneur because we might poke out an eye.

Like helicopter parents, gremlins love us and don't want to see us get hurt. Their messages get lost in translation because all we can see is their holding us back.

So first calm the chatter down, so that your rational mind can talk. Relaxation response the heck out of this gremlin. When you feel the response, ask yourself, what's the worst that can happen? Will you actually lose an eye from starting a coaching business? Since I'm a new coach and can't afford to have my reptilian brain surgically removed, what new message do I want the gremlin to say (Schneider, 2010)?

It's pretty cool to have a built-in feedback system whose sole mission is caring for our safety. But it's a clunker like the Millennium Falcon. So it takes a brilliant person to understand it, right Client Solo?

Chapter Five
EXCITE YOUR TRIBE

"Future superstars don't get there by keeping part of their heart in reserve."
—John Eliot

With your signature strengths being fully utilized and your gremlins accepting their reassignment to being your cheerleaders, it's time to fully engage in serving others, the company of people who share your values, your tribe.

As you shift your focus from internal work to external service, the gameful framework still applies but with a different perspective. As the creator of your tribe, take ownership of the objectives and rules. Create feedback loops through reinforcement— especially as you celebrate your clients' achievements. And by clearly stating the problem you are addressing, you will naturally attract the ideal clients to choose to enroll in your coaching services.

Don't mistake "exciting your tribe" for being some motivational entertainer who only works their tribe into euphoric states of jubilation. There is a time and place for those things, but sole reliance on it leads to an unrealistic Pollyanna form of happiness.

Challenge promotes growth. Do not take away the "privilege of the struggle" from your client. Know that to excite your tribe, you'll play the role of provocateur, agitator, and energizer. Use your curiosity to create zones for awakening and trusting discomfort.

Class 11: Recognize the Nature of Relationships

"Instead, we comfort ourselves with feelings of moral superiority. We tell ourselves that we are above engaging in conflict over unimportant trifles. But despite what we think, we turn the other cheek. Not because it is right, but because it is easy."

—Chin-Ning Chu

Without a client, you are not a coach. With all the tools you've acquired from training programs and education, there is still a relational aspect of this profession that's quintessential to the coaching process. Like life itself, there's dynamism, successions of ups and downs and all-arounds, in which a client delves deeper and deeper to reach more significant levels of clarity and self-actualization. This is their game of life, and we're all their supporting actors. Through substantial questions, you create the space and the axis. By setting their own agenda, the client provides the inertia for the wheel to spin.

There is something magical about this process. But the magic is more universal than unique. Just as a person called to pave roads takes the utmost pride in knowing millions of people will traverse the streets that they built, a coach doesn't need to make any more spectacular the relationship they have with their clients than the calling in and of itself. Coaching, as a relational profession, requires one to engage with different types of relationships and to show up in various ways. I'll explain this in the proceeding tiny little classes in this chapter.

Before we can even begin to talk about ways to excite your tribe, you must understand the very nature of relationships. Aristotle breaks them down into three categories: the useful, the pleasurable, and the virtuous. Useful relationships are based strictly on the utility that one person can provide another. We see this all the time in the exchange of goods and services. Without the exchange, there is no relationship. Pleasurable relationships are very similar in that there's an exchange of hedonic elements in the relationship. This shows up in the hanging out with friends who have mutual interests or in the hookup culture at colleges. We encounter these less frequently than useful relationships but more regularly than virtuous ones. In the third relationship, you wish what's best for the other person regardless of the usefulness (or the lack thereof) or the pleasure that the relationship brings to you (Aristotle, 2009).

As coaching is a relational profession, the concepts that deal with the other relationships in your life can also be applied to your coaching practice. Every calling has an aspect of service, but if you genuinely want to solidify yourself as a full-time coach, you cannot ignore the utilitarian nature of coaching. This does not mean creating coach-client relationships that are devoid of levity or goodwill. Whether your coaching hours are billable or whether they are pro bono and going to your International Coaching Federation (ICF) certification hours, you're keeping score in some way, shape or form. That's essential to living gamefully. Having your clients have a "stake in the game" through investing in themselves is also a necessary part of their becoming antifragile, which will be discussed later in this book. You serve and belong to multiple tribes. Chances are that if you are considering coaching with a steadier, full-time income, you want the freedom of time and resources that allow you to serve your family and community.

As a coach, you respect the best interest of your clients. As a seasoned coach, you must be tenacious as your client's wheel of life spins. As an unapologetic coach, you respect the utilitarian nature of your coach-client relationship.

You are mixing business with friendships, and it is vital in networking that you are upfront with close friends and coaching colleagues about your most exact intentions. So many times people will unintentionally feign a virtuous friendship and offer to coach at no cost, as a way to preserve "face." If you genuinely don't expect something in return from someone, erase your coaching service from your mind. But if there's any form of payment or barter, simply acknowledge that you are about to go into a conversation on usefulness and exchange.

Class 12: Attract Your Ideal Clients

"Here comes your man."
—**The Pixies**

From elevator speeches to catchy tag lines, freebies to email lists, drawing people into your tribe and communicating with them— these are creative skills that can only be crafted over time and with consistency.

You can use intricate auto-responders and flashy freebies to get people to join your tribe, but how many leads are actually engaging with you after opting-in? Your list can sometimes be an illusion of success. Eliminate your friends and family from your list. Take out the percentage who only subscribed for the freebie. Now remove the list of people who can actually pay for your services. This may be a more accurate representation of your warm leads.

Everyone on your list can be of value, as you want to get any person who hears about you to do one primary thing: understand exactly what it is that you do. Once they know what you really do as a coach (not how you do it), the ball is in their court to either become a client or make referrals for you. So even if they don't need your coaching services, they may be able to refer a client to you.

Consistently market your coaching services, and your list will grow. And as your audience gets larger, you may be thinking of a communication strategy to effectively connect to each member of your audience. Should you communicate differently to different demographic segments? Do you change your strategies depending on the medium you're using? To a certain extent, segments matter (especially if your mission serves multiple) and your communication will be different depending on the platform. You can't give a five-point speech on Instagram. You can, however, identify and conceptualize your ideal client and use a simple communication strategy called A.I.D.A. to peak their interest.

Conceptualize your ideal client.

Every person's unique experience is a blend of their external environment, their internal world, and a universe that is too immense for any individual to grasp. It's time to visualize your ideal client. Take out a piece of paper and write down all the demographic information that you can. Be specific and don't put down ranges. An *actual* person is not 25 - 60 years old. What is their job status? How long have they worked in their job? Where do they live? What is their family status? This is your ideal client's external environment.

Dig deeper. Do they consider their work a job, a career, or a calling? What gets them out of bed in the morning? What do they struggle with? If they could wave a magic wand and change one/any aspect of their life, what would they change? Why would they change it? What emotions are they feeling as a result of their struggle? What emotions do they want to feel? This is your client's internal world.

As for the ideal client's universe, this is the immense matrix of data, energy, and information that we all share. It represents Truth, which no one person will ever know fully. By stepping back and listening empathetically, we can create space for our clients to connect with Truth, which leads to the powerful transformative growth experience. The Truth can be that there are others experiencing their challenge and the result would be less loneliness. Or that an assumption they were making about being ostracized by their family for doing their own thing was false.

Notice that identifying your ideal client doesn't entail *you*, your amazing five-point system, or your ground-breaking book. In fact, if your ideal client could make their pain go away without having breakthrough sessions or a three-month package, they'd do it in a heartbeat. While you may be charismatic and empowering, your ideal client is ultimately engaging with you on a *utilitarian* basis. They are exchanging goods for a service. With your ideal client at the forefront, you can now communicate with them using a simple, effective strategy, A.I.D.A.

Use the A.I.D.A. technique to communicate with your ideal client.

A.I.D.A. stands for *Attention. Interest. Desire. Action.*

- Step 1. Different triggers get people's *attention*. What draws *your* ideal client's attention? Is it alarm? Or that they know, like, and trust you? Do they perk up when they hear about boosting their power and prestige?
- Step 2. *Interest* takes attention and draws in your ideal client further. It backs it up with statistics, theories, or stories.

- Step 3. By *desire*, I'm talking about the possibilities of living a life without a particular challenge and what the benefits might look like.
- Step 4. You are directing your ideal client to have a call to *action*.

Now putting this all together. Use A.I.D.A. to communicate to your ideal client. Whether it's a speech, a video, or an email, it all works in the same way. Use the ideal client write-up as the back-story to clearly communicate to them.

So for example, let's say that my client is a new coach looking to generate leads:

Attention: You'll never need to use another communication system again.

Interest: Even the most seasoned coaches, do not have a clear communication strategy. This results in:

- Wasting time and effort through unclear communication to your email lists.
- Having complicated strategies for each platform, which become antiquated as soon as emergent platforms show up.
- Red hot leads that are utterly confused with what the coach is doing.

As you are building your business, now is not the time for people to be unclear about what you do and who you serve.

Desire: As you perfect this system, you'll attract the perfect client willing to pay a premium for your coaching services.

Action: Subscribe now and I'll show you how to do it in five steps.

I didn't mention the back-story. I didn't talk about how cool I am. I didn't talk about my empirically tested process. I simply hit their pain point, built their interest, painted a picture of what life might be like without the pain, and gave a call to action. Depending on the level of investment, you'll have to modify the length, the benefits, and why you are the best to coach them. But it all comes back to this simple model.

It's also helpful when you have content blocks to imagine what your ideal client is experiencing at the moment and send your contacts an email, make a video, or even write a book. I had a client-coach try to identify her ideal client and use the A.I.D.A. technique. In less than two weeks, she had her first paid client.

Once you've attracted and enrolled your ideal clients, it's time to serve the *beejezus* out of them. You serve them by showing up for them in the different capacities they need to grow and feel supported. This means that what they need won't always be the same. You will have to learn to engage in the various aspects of yourself that allow you to encourage someone's growth and support them in the process. I find, typically, this leads me to show up in three primary ways: as The Lover, The Trickster, and The Great Dictator.

Class 13: You are the Lover

"The soul must always stand ajar, ready to welcome the ecstatic experience."
—Emily Dickinson

Love is the ultimate human emotion. Between two people, strangers or soulmates, a shared connection over a positive emotion can occur in a micro-moment. Like life itself, it grows and dies. The love can last a lifetime of micro-moments or just one hot American summer of micro-moments.

When you think about the connection with your client, what is it except for your loving on the highest level of Aristotelian relationships? When your client is suffering, you offer compassion. When they experience great joys, you celebrate. Session to session, micro-moment to micro-moment, you share a connection with your client and respond to them with love.

Fredrickson (2013) has shown the effects of love to enhance neural coupling, which influences communication and understanding. Oxytocin levels increase to strengthen trust and cooperation. And the connection between the brain and heart grows stronger through the vagus nerve. So while your heart does not skip a beat every time we meet, the vagal pathway does trip out.

Just like finding one daily thing for which to be grateful can change your mindset, finding one daily micro-moment that you choose for love to be your prevailing desire with a *new* person can change the way you relate with everyone in your life. As an introvert, this is difficult for me as I enjoy solitary tasks. Or it may be difficult for you if you have felt burned in the past, but you don't have to *go for broke* with every person with whom you engage. Tribe or not, engage with someone with the purpose of sharing positive emotions in that moment. Look for synchrony between you and the other person. A mutual laugh or smile is enough for neural coupling, oxytocin increasing, and the vagal pathway opening. Look for the mutual motive to invest in each other's well-being through mutual care.

Within your tribe, love each member into fulfilling their highest purpose with the elements of teaching, parenting, and healing. But more importantly, allow reciprocity to keep you in the state of a learner, a child, and the wounded. And when it's time for a member of your tribe to fly, take pride in the fact that you played an instrumental role in their outgrowing your nest.

The greatest non-secret to the way of the unapologetic coach is to love.

To be a coach is to be a lover.

Class 14. You are the Trickster and the Fool

"Look up, Hannah. The soul of man has been given wings, and at last he is beginning to fly. He is flying into the rainbow— into the light of hope, into the future, the glorious future that belongs to you, to me, and to all of us."
—**The Barber**, The Great Dictator

Be a sinner and a saint within another person's tribe. But when you are nurturing one, play the trickster and the fool. We have been indoctrinated to think that failure is attributed to weakness. So living safely, not taking chances or putting yourself out there is status quo. Contrastingly, vulnerability is so punk rock right now. Yet with all the TED talks and books on the topic, who wants to admit to someone that they have challenges?

If you think that your ideal client wants to engage with you, then you still believe that the man in the red suit delivers gifts on Christmas Eve. We go to the mall and sit on his lap because that's the way to the presents! The man in the red suit is the trickster. And just because all of this is done with a wink and a nod, doesn't make the awe of my son opening a present on Christmas morning any less inspiring.

Harry Houdini was also a trickster. He demonstrated how a trick was done and then fascinated you by actually doing it. As a coach, you do the opposite. You perform the trick with your clients, and then you show them how you did it so that they can do it for themselves and others (if that is the sort of coach you are). Houdini warned us of frauds that would use these techniques to hoodwink us. Nevertheless, just because it's not magic, doesn't make it less magical.

Be critical of your homemade process of transformation. And continue to streamline the mechanism for which it brings the change that your clients desperately desire. Be your best skeptic. And always do no harm. Build feedback loops to improve and streamline the process. And limit your platitudes.

If you are a life coach, ground yourself in empirical studies and theory. It's like sawing your assistant in half and *not* knowing how the trick is performed. Don't be afraid to say that your solution is nothing less than the placebo effect. Because to create a space for your client to wander and dance is the most beautiful thing you can do.

You become the conduit for transformation. You are not the transformation. You become the conduit for healing. You are not the healer. You become the conduit for magic. You are not the magician (Dierolf, Meier, & Szabo, 2009).

As a coach, someone has entrusted you with their innermost dreams and insecurities. They seem paradoxical, but you offer no solutions. This seems counterintuitive because our egos want to provide solutions to our clients immediately. You are the fool in the king's court. You can simultaneously be a provocateur, appreciative inquirer, and empathetic listener. You co-explore with clients the secret passageways between their personal hell and heaven, and it's your inner trickster that allows you to move fluidly between these spaces (Hyde, 2017). Plato would ask you what's beyond the shadows on the wall that you claim to be your reality. Is there life outside of the caves in which we live? The trickster shows up as Morpheus in the Matrix and asks Neo to make a choice.

In business, you are the go-between rigid strategic plans and pure improvisation. You are a complex adaptive system, the equivalent of a masterful jazz performance.

To be the trickster is to be curious. To be a coach is to be a trickster.

Class 15: You are the Great Dictator

"Listen."
—**Hannah**, The Great Dictator

Reciprocity, curiosity, assuming paradoxical roles, gameplay and above all, love, precede owning your role as the great dictator of your tribe. This is your business, and you design and enforce the rules of play. As a spectator, you get a front row seat to witness personal transformation and you are creating the boundaries.

The greatest (not to be mixed with "the most infamous") follow their own rules of servant leadership to craft a community of genuine care. These four components have been studied cross-culturally (McMillan & Chavis, 1986) and will now be condensed for you to individualize and practice.

Membership

Membership creates a psychological sense of safety using barriers to entry, boundaries, and common symbols. Anything that delineates the in-group from the out-group is a form of membership. Application forms, fees, participation in an activity, logos, and slogans— these are all tactics used to create psychological safety. In online groups, these come in the form of user agreements. Most common agreements require no personal promotion in groups. In my Facebook group, I simply tell the adults something like, "Don't be a dolt." I am the arbiter. I have final say. If someone even comes close to disturbing the sanctity of a safe community, I ban them without explanation.

Influence

You can make your influence on the group as apparent as you want, but to keep a member, they must feel as if they have influence over the group. This is a mark of all great, not infamous, dictators. A cybernetic feedback loop transforms a tribe into a self-sustaining organization. The feeling that each member influences their group gives cohesion. When the organization is ready, create mentoring systems or orientation programs to transition new members and give senior members influence. You solely don't have to be in charge of message control once someone knows, likes, and trusts your coaching business. Do not misinterpret the idea of influence as hiring people to do the work you don't know how to do.

Fulfillment of Needs

The fulfillment of needs has a direct correlation to the clarity with which a client can articulate their pain and the service that you provide to coach them as they grow. As the great dictator, you must make obvious the micro-, meso-, and macro-benefits of engaging with you and the tribe. You created the rules through membership, participation in the group is voluntary with the feeling of influence, and a feedback loop is established for each member through the fulfillment of needs. In coaching, this can simply be you asking the client, "What was your biggest takeaway from this session?"

Shared Connection

A shared connection can come in two ways. The first comes from history. The longer and more detailed the history, the easier it is to share a connection. The Catholic Church uses symbols and rituals in its history so much that you can travel to almost any part of the world and feel an almost immediate sense of belonging whether you're at the Vatican or some progressive rock mass in Tampa. In your branding, what is the story that you are telling? Who are your champions who will give your testimonials? All of this builds on the foundation of your tribe.

The second way to build a shared connection is through intense experiences, otherwise known as high valence experiences. Retreats or trainings are the best examples. From the micro-second a person steps onto the retreat site, you can create a sensory experience that brings out a peak performance response from the participant. With respect to people who went to actual war, the phrase "we went to war together" will be used to describe the support from a cohort going through a retreat, or graduate school, or any particularly highly emotional, or valent, time.

As the great dictator creates history— highly powerful experiences through retreats (yes, moments to experience love, if you read tiny little class 13)— and honors influence, upholds membership and fulfills individual needs, the tribe becomes its own ecosystem. It grows and contracts like a living organism.

Just like our bodies are full of harmonious micro-ecosystems, so is the world. It is not your goal to be the sole dictator, but merely to excite and feed your tribe. Understand and meet their needs with the knowledge that thousands of other eco-systems exist, each with their own great dictators. As someone exits your tribe, they are the perfect fit to serve or lead another. The great dictator's role is important, and it completely lacks egotism.

To be a coach is to be a great dictator.

Chapter Six
INITIATE LASTING CHANGE

"Everyone who has ever taken a shower has had an idea. It's the person who gets out of the shower, dries off, and does something about it that makes a difference."
—Nolan Bushnell

Y ou are to be commended as you are reaching a point of no return. *Initiating lasting change* is an element containing multiple facets. The chapter is correspondingly the longest. In this chapter, you'll be targeting your penultimate goal above all other, not just goals for mini-games. If you haven't done so already, you will be making a declaration soon. And you will have a growing tribe and virtuous friends who love and support you. In this chapter vision becomes action.

The non-virtuous will love your declaration for other reasons. You become the fodder for ignominy. And when, not if, you fall short of expectations, they'll parade around your ostensible failure like a carcass proving why others should never operate out of self-concordance.

This is a tactic to elicit fear, not love. It causes soul paralysis and your pursuit of status-quo-concordant goals. And in the game of life, since progression and digression are both movement, the only "game over" is stagnation.

Your critics will say it's impossible until you do it. When you do it, they'll copy you.

Step to the edge, unapologetic coach, despite the fear. Your wins and losses have emotional consequences. When things are working, enjoy the elation. When they are not working, know the pain will pass. Your worth is infinitely greater than the sum of your accomplishments and failures. Despite the outcome, your entire life has been a dress rehearsal for this moment. Learn from it and perform again. Raise your bar and perform again.

This is the core of the self-fulfilling prophecy. It is not a covert wish, but a perpetual performance and action. It's a cycle in which you have high expectations in your beliefs and motivation in the short term.

Contrastingly, have low expectations for your actual performance. Having low expectations will naturally lead you to ask, "What did I learn from this experience?" And begin the cycle, the rehearsal, again.

It is the perspective of the realistic optimist. And it has its benefits on everything from the immune system to resilience to longevity and success in all domains (Bandura, 1997).

Class 16: Distinguish between Job, Career, and Calling

> *"If a man is called to be a street sweeper, he should sweep streets even as a Michelangelo painted, or Beethoven composed music or Shakespeare wrote poetry. He should sweep streets so well that all the hosts of heaven and earth will pause to say, 'Here lived a great street sweeper who did his job well.'"*
>
> **—Martin Luther King**

I wrestled with work as job, career, or calling so many times, and every time I submitted to its existential *reverse chicken wing* finishing move. Either I'd throw in the towel and force myself to acquiesce to other people's expectations of me, or I'd become so overwhelmed with the insatiability with privileges and accolades that I thought there was no solution to being on the existential hamster wheel. In retrospect, it was Dr. Keyes's notion of settling and striving in the context of my lived experience.

The most frequent statement I've heard around this topic over the past 15 years is this: "There's got to be something more to life than this." There's got to be something more to life than … what? To *settling*? To *striving*? To chasing the idea of something?

This statement was most likely the impetus for your desire to coach. If you asked it, chances are that you are not functioning at the most optimal capacity or feeling amazing doing it. But being unsettled or striving is not a sign of anything except your readiness for profound growth. Let's use a perspective strategy to understand the work you're currently doing and where you want to go.

For classification purposes, Amy Wrzesniewski and her colleagues (1999) define three categories in which we perceive and thus show up to work: Job, Career, and Calling.

Work as a Job: Work as a job is approaching your work as a means to an end. Your interests are outside of your occupation. You look forward to retirement. This is where you'll hear your clients saying things like, "They can't *pay* me enough to do that!"

Work as a Career: Work as career is approaching your current work as a means of upward mobility. Your interest is in promotion and prestige. And that's what you look forward to the most.

Work as a Calling: Work as calling is the feeling that your work is fully integrated with your deepest values and strengths. There is no "fake it until you make it." And you're not thinking about retiring or prestige, but rather, how valuable the calling is to you and the people you serve.

So unless your dream job from 20 years ago changes along with your skills and experience, you will outgrow it. The more you live your life, the more you will be presented with what you "can" be. And thus, you must be. What were once callings became jobs. So, is there something more to life than this? If it's a job, it can become your career. If it's a career, it can become your calling. And thus, to live gamefully is to understand that as you level-up, your capacity increases in volume. Your goal is to fill it. Your blade sharpens and becomes more useful. And it is not a meaningless cycle of starting over, but rather, playing with new skills and new challenges.

The benefits of pursuing a calling orientation include a higher satisfaction with life and a more significant allowance to integrate your strengths into your craft. Now if you find yourself in a job orientation, do you have personally satisfying activities outside of your job that are in alignment with your values? If coaching allows you the highest satisfaction outside of work, revel in the notion that this has the potential to be your calling orientation when the utilitarian aspects of coaching align.

Class 17: Self-Concordance

"A million voices pulling you in a million different directions, which one is yours?"
—Gregory Ellison

Imagine swimming upstream with maximum effort. Think about the distance you'd cover. Now, reverse stream. Keep the same intensity and visualize yourself swimming with the same effort downstream. You cover a lot more distance. You get to your destination faster. You don't even have to work as hard to get to your destination. This is what happens when you set goals that align with your interests and values. They are also called self-concordant goals.

Committing to self-concordant goals benefits your client (Spence & Oades, 2011) and you as you live gamefully. There are three components that make a goal self-concordant. First, you must feel competent that you have the skills to achieve the task. Second, you freely choose to go after the goal. Third, you feel accepted and loved by those important to you for pursuing your goals. This is why getting someone's "blessing" is truly meaningful to so many of us.

I struggled with this one for a while. As a neuroscience/pre-med undergrad, I had the skills to pay the bills. I had two parents who were physicians. So I had their blessing, but I didn't feel as though I was deciding to be a doctor. It was much more extrinsic. It eventually became a theme in my life, as I desperately wanted to be an individual without apologizing to the collective.

Now if you meet the criterion for a self-concordant goal, things become easier. The choices around you are energizing.

It's easier to get out of bed on your worst days because you want to go on this adventure, as opposed to having to go on it. As you start achieving these goals, your well-being goals up, internal conflicts get resolved, and your motivation surges. You start to ride an upward spiral of joy and moxie. Even if you have obligations that are not in total alignment with your goals, pursuing your self-concordant goals even a few hours a week will start the upward spiral going in all aspects of your life (Sheldon & Elliot, 1999).

Goals are not created equal. So choose wisely.

Class 18: Find Your Big, Hairy, Audacious Goal

"We choose to go to the moon in this decade and do the other things, not because they are easy, but because they are hard."

—**John F. Kennedy**

You are built to take on challenges. Studies show people consistently choose less paid challenging tasks over better paid boring tasks. It may not feel so, but it is a privilege for you to have the choice to take on the challenge of launching your coaching business.

It's time to clarify what gets you and your ideal self out of bed in the mornings. This is a goal that's *big*, as it has a long-term vision. It's the umbrella under which your other goals align. It inspires, motivates, and speaks to your deepest purpose.

This is a goal that's *hairy* like a night yeti. It's challenging, scary, and will require nothing less than a maximum effort.

It is *audacious*, as it is defiant of popular convention, and draws skepticism from others.

Setting *big hairy audacious goals* (BHAGs) are common among one-person organizations and nations alike, because they motivate everyone within the organization when used correctly. As you set up your dream target, it is of primary importance to find a goal that leaves you awestruck. Merely wanting relief is not a BHAG because it's not inspiring. Your BHAG is your dream manifest.

What is your BHAG?

Make it clear and tangible, so you can write it down and know clearly when you've hit the target? Don't worry if you can't articulate it in your first draft. This is also where working with your coach is most helpful.

Fast forward to the day that you've finally achieved the goal. Where will you be? What time of the year is it? Is it day or night? How does it feel to reach your BHAG? What are you going to do now? How will you celebrate? Take in a deep breath, close your eyes, and feel the accomplishment as you exhale.

Do this often and get more specific every time. Write it down and read it to yourself. Make the scenes more vivid. Envision all of your senses and emotions when you are living your dream come true.

The more you engage in this activity, the more your brain thinks your goal has been achieved. You feel less of Maslow's stretch, as there is less cognitive dissonance in your mind. It becomes easier to focus, prioritize and, yes, get out of bed. But tantamount to BHAGs and visioning is being smart and getting real. Onward and upward!

Class 19: Be SMART. Get Real.

"Necessity is the mother of invention."
—**Plato**

It's time to take your target and paint a bullseye on it. In using the game framework, you need the bullseye and concentric circles to give you a feedback loop necessary to make adjustments as you aim and shoot for your target goals.

Having goals that are specific, measurable, achievable, realistic (even if challenging), and time-bound (SMART) is the standard criterion for creating goals with feedback mechanisms built in.

Don't fall into the trap of just creating SMART goals without being inspired by your BHAG first. This is a surefire way to get stuck on the hedonic treadmill, strive aimlessly, or settle in the rat race.

Take this to the next level by preparing for any inner hindrances, gremlins, and turmoil that may happen during the process. This is called mental contrasting. As you identify every internal block, create an action to counteract the block. This is called implementation intent. Getting real through mental contrasting and implementation intentions (MMII) is one of the most powerful ways to achieve your *big hairy audacious goals* (Oettingen & Gollwitzer, 2010). The terminology is much more complex than the actual practice. As you identify each hindrance, put it into an "if..." statement and create your intention by answering with an "then I will..." statement. If "hindrance" occurs, then "I will take this specific action." Not only are you simulating what you want in the future, but you are going through every possible scenario that may stop you internally from achieving it.

Here's a short example:

Goal:

Get 7 ideal clients at $2,500 each this month

Mental Contrast:

Anxiety to call lead

Blanking out during the call

Dream client is perfect except they don't have the financial resources

Implementation Intention:

If I get anxiety to call a lead, then I will use the five-second rule and call.

If I blank out during a call, then I will make sure my sales script is in front of me and stay curious.

If I meet a dream client who is a perfect fit except they don't have the financial resources, then I will understand the utilitarian nature of the relationship and know that giving the service away may actually hurt their progress.

Class 20: Declare and Commit

"Necessity is the mother of invention."
—Plato

Your emergence as an unapologetic coach can appear as if you were reborn overnight. But in the deep recesses of night, you probably began a clandestine journey. Or perhaps the beginning of your coach training was an addendum to your current job. If you started your journey in secret, without telling anyone, no one could criticize you if you failed. If you continue to keep this a side project, you always have something fall back on.

While the practicality of having a job that serves your basic needs is important, there is a problem. The more you transform into the unapologetic coach, the smaller your world becomes. The more notoriety you gain. The transformation will be impossible to keep a secret. You will radiate confidence as you reach your ideal self. Furthermore, your ostensible failures will be in front of a larger audience.

Be careful not to gain a reputation as the dabbler coach— one who cannot commit to their truest passions. You will be passed up for coaches who don't dabble and are committed to their craft, even if you have an array of coaching skills. Inevitably, on your coaching business journey, you will come across as a seemingly unscalable, impenetrable wall. The dabbler coach will run off in fear of being seen as a failure.

You, the unapologetic coach, take your knapsack and throw it over the wall. Your necessity to get to the other side exponentially raises your willpower and your waypower— for example, your ability to find different solutions when obstacles arise.

Your imagination only limits you. As trees become ladders, unassuming rocks scream to become tools, and your clothes become ropes.

As you commit to throwing your knapsack over the way, self-perception becomes alive as spectators see your confidence. Your inner self-confidence boosts as well, as you have made a declaration to get to the other side and keep moving toward your vision (Ben-Shahar, 2017).

Class 21: Chunk It Down

"When eating an elephant take one bite at a time."
—**Creighton Abrams**

So you've taken your vision and made a declaration. You're motivated. You're real. And you know you're going to need to be creative about getting through your obstacles. You've created your first goal that's specific, measurable, and time-bound, and it has a minimum standard built into the feedback loop so that you know when to proceed to your next big goal. With this first goal, it's important on many levels that you hit your target. To do this, "chunk down" goals— break them into smaller goals that contribute to the main goal. Each chunk can be "chunked down" even further. Continue to chunk down until you have an action step that can be knocked out in less than a day. If your schedule is packed, chunk it down so it can be knocked out in less than an hour. The goal of an action step is to meet your skill set and to achieve it, at most, in one day. It's the same cognitive process that we use to understand the world without being overwhelmed.

You have to chunk down in a way that makes sense for you. Here is an example:

Let's say that you want to transition full-time in 18 months with three straight months of signing four $2000 clients to three-month packages. As you work your current job and grow your nest egg, you have allocated 20 hours a week for starting your business— marketing, coaching, follow-up, and administrative work (St Laurent).

Chunk down to 9 months: Perhaps this goal looks like five clients signed for a three-month package at $775 each.

Chunk down to three months: You may want to have your system of breakthrough calls in place, and you're getting three new calls a week. Your goal is to sign one out of ten for $775 for a three-month package.

Chunk down to one month from today: Small systems and templates are in place to capture leads. You're offering free coaching for three sessions for a testimonial and the possibility of upgrading to a paid three-month package.

One week from today: You know your ideal client and contacted ten people who might be the ideal client about the possibility of coaching them. You launched your Facebook group for ideal clients.

Today: Spend an hour documenting your ideal client and why you are the ideal coach to serve them. Send to Marc Cordon and a few other coaches for their feedback. Spend an hour creating a Facebook group.

The cool thing about having a feedback loop (the absolute minimum outcome) is that you know when to proceed. So if you meet a minimum outcome sooner, move to the next goal.

Make your actions easy so that it's hard for you or your gremlin to pass judgment on your worth as an emerging coach. Either you do it, or you don't.

If that's still overwhelming, shoot me an email. I'm happy to serve.

Class 22: Engage in Deep Work

"Who you are, what you think, feel, and do, what you love— is the sum of what you focus on."
—Cal Newport

Your action steps are set up like a kick. Stand. Raise foot. Extend leg. Put foot down. Now you can turn up the music, play words with friends and kick the air, and check it off your list. That's a fun game. Or you can learn proper form so that you don't injure yourself. Then stand in front of a tree and strike it with so much force that it snaps. This is deep work.

It is complete engagement and commitment to your task no matter how small it seems. Completely creating an environment for absolute focus. Yes, it entails turning off the internet and fully emerging yourself in your environment. If we create space for our clients to have deep discoveries, we should do ourselves the same favor. Also, keep a place for your chatter, as it will appear.

In working with my coach on how to do deep work, I have a log of my work, but I also have a stack of post-it notes for my chatter to come out. These thoughts and ideas have no value to achieving the task at hand, but they always feel like divine sparks of creativity that I might not get back. Instead of storing them in my mind, I write the ideas on a post-it and drop them in an unused bento box. Every two weeks, I'll open the bento box for an hour, enter the ideas, and look over old ones. It is an endless source of inspiration and content for copy when I get stuck (Newport, 2016).

Class 23: Pound the Rock

"Ritualize to actualize."
—**James Kerr**

Routinize as much as you as you possibly can. If you think that creating standard operating procedures takes away any of the sexiness of your fantastic future or the sheer boldness of making a declaration, you might want to reconsider. Routinization makes goal achievement more achievable.

Your brain is a mission-driven machine. Schedule recurring times for deep work and goal achievement to happen. Even block accordingly. So, Mondays from 9 a.m. to noon, you're responding to leads and writing copy. Two clients in the afternoon (or space for two clients), and then time for family. Build it into your circadian rhythm.

This is tough when you're struggling to find your ideal client and working a full-time job because you'll almost take whoever, whenever. This will change. When I first started up, my ideal clients would have rigid schedules on Wall Street (there went my Saturday night). I had a client in Asia (goodbye Tuesdays at 1 a.m.). I had an excellent client who worked so many jobs that I just told her to text me when she was free, and I'd call her back if I had a slot open. This had less to do with my flexibility and more to do with my desperation to hold onto and find new clients.

You're an entrepreneur. Don't give up all of your agency, your awareness that you can create change in the world, in this transition. Bend, but don't break yourself.

Another part of your standard operating procedure is creating templates that work for you and your business. Using A.I.D.A. for your copy is a template that's widely used for marketing, but if it doesn't work for you, create a process. Standardize your closing call outline, your welcome emails, and contract, so you only need to make a few adjustments. Even if 80 percent of your work is standardized, 20 percent of your time is more than enough to innovate and improvise.

Class 24: Make Little Changes Leading to Major Improvements

"All changes, even positive ones, are scary. Attempts to reach goals through radical or revolutionary means often fail because they heighten fear. But the small steps of kaizen disarm the brain's fear response, stimulating rational thought and creative play."
—Robert Maurer

Action steps are continually moving you towards your goal. Kaizen is the mindset that minor improvements lead to significant changes. The effect of kaizen is not additive, but exponential. If you commit to even 1 percent growth a day, you won't see the changes at first, but like any spiral, growth compounds.

It is the same strategy that both Coach John Wooden and Toyota used to create sustainable, dominant organizations.

Kaizen translated into your coaching business is gradually changing the rules. For example, you have decided that Mondays from 3 p.m. to 4 p.m., you are writing copy to your email list. Your goal is about 250 words. After four weeks, can you cut off five minutes? Can you eventually kaizen this to 15 minutes?

The 45 extra minutes isn't meant for you to stop. Take a breath. And move to the next most important action item that you have chunked down. Continue your deep work on your next task.

Class 25: Earn Your Moxie

"Self-concept is self-destiny."
—**Nathaniel Braden**

Don't believe the fairy-tale that the most successful individuals were born with an unfair advantage, amount of moxie, capabilities for learning (real or perceived), or performance of designated tasks (Bandura, 1997). If you read autobiographies of the most successful businesspersons, they commonly pushed forward and took steps toward their dreams despite having low confidence or high fear.

The most profound way to boost your moxie is through consistent action. The more deep work in which you engage, the more likely you are to experience more success and more failure.

If you treat your successes and failures like "dress rehearsals," you can improve before your next performance.

With success comes feelings of satisfaction and short-term happiness boosts. This reinforces your initial beliefs to take action, and your motivation rises. The more successes you celebrate, the more your moxie elevates. You will have a higher motivation to engage in deeper work in your coaching business.

Your moxie is a gremlin repellent. It will give you permission to fail or be imperfect. You'll realize that you were blowing your gremlins out of proportion. So if an unexpected turn does happen, your moxie helps you to know that the ramifications are not nearly as severe as they could have been.

Chapter Seven

EVOLVE AN ANTIFRAGILE MINDSET

"I am burning. If anyone lacks tinder, let him set his rubbish ablaze with my fire."

—Rumi

P sychological flexibility, adaptability, resilience, grit—all have the implication of withstanding disorder but to a varying degree can only withstand so much. Just as a lack of disease does not mean the presence of well-being, we need to understand the limitations that language can put on varying levels of fragility. Eventually things break down. The fragile crumble quickly. The resilient can withstand more, but eventually break down.

The notion of antifragility suggests a truer polarity on the continuum of a response to stressors. As we embrace failure, we bounce back faster. But at some point we become impervious to the stressor. And at some point beyond that we become stronger as a result of the stressor (Taleb, 2012).

You know that part of *Wicked* right before intermission, where Elphaba realizes just how powerful she is and starts hovering over the townsfolk? That's antifragility. It's a game changer to your mindset. You are beyond bulletproof. You are a hydra that sprouts two heads for every one that is cut off. It's beyond resilience. It's beyond adaptation. And in the gaming world, you suddenly realize that you have an unfair advantage.

As a coach, you look forward to failing a certification test as the feedback just makes you a stronger coach. You look forward to discovery calls and see that clients are not a good fit for you. If ICF was the Nintendo universe, this is the part in *Super-Mario Bros* where an invincibility star pops out of the pipe and you start running around like a crazy person. It's the part of *Pac-Man* where you get the Power Pellets and go on the offensive with the ghosts that used to haunt you. Like everything in nature, dissonance will return to homeostasis. In other words, the potency of the invincibility stars and power pellets wanes. So while you have this unfair advantage, it's time to embrace antifragility. Antifragility is not false bravado or fearlessness. In a few pages, I'll make the distinction between the egoist and the egotist. Huge difference.

Class 26: Take Extreme Ownership

"Until you take ownership for your life, you will always be chasing happiness."
—**Sean Stephenson**

Hold yourself always fully accountable for everything in your world— both the successes and failures. Blaming of any sort demonstrates a lack of extreme ownership.

Victim consciousness has no place in your business. While comforting, victim consciousness allows you to disengage from personal responsibility. By taking extreme ownership, not only are you shifting useless enervating energy to the creative, but you are fully taking responsibility for the way you shape the world. One hundred percent accountability means that your *practice of agency* is meeting your *potential of agency*. This puts the future in your hands and only your hands.

Like other techniques, this one automatically builds a growth mindset. Regardless of a particular result, holding yourself accountable for outcomes allows you to identify areas of improvement the next time. No matter what happens, everything can be tinkered and improved by your hands. Look forward with excitement and appreciation, because this is how you will become beyond resilient. It is how you become antifragile. Remember, it's all a dress rehearsal, baby!

As your business grows, you'll be presented with opportunities that are fully in your control— and some that are out of it. Make sure you create a plan to "pound the rock" daily for at least a year. You will create a strong business foundation this way. And it is in your full control.

As your moxie rises and you gain notoriety, others may talk about collaborations or ask you to speak on their book tours. These are out of your control. While they should be considered, handle these conversations *outside* of your deep work schedule using the barbell strategy (Class 31). Even the best-laid plans can fall through, and you never want your failure or success to be at another person's hands.

As you listen to their ideas, allow yourself to feel the excitement and feel grateful that your work is being recognized. These are some of the feelings you may have identified in your BHAG visioning. Never assume that anything will result in your *big break*. Your being discovered, your *big break*, will come from consistent hard work with your voice turned to 11. Don't set yourself up to blame others, as you'll start making decisions from a place of desperation.

Class 27: Play with Something to Lose

"Twenty years from now you will be more disappointed by the things you didn't do than by the ones you did do.

So throw off the bowlines. Sail away from the safe harbor. Catch the trade winds in your sails. Explore. Dream. Discover."

—Mark Twain

You may be in a situation in which you have generated a tremendous rapport in your current occupation. You can leave work early or take a day off without ramification, while other less-seasoned colleagues do not have the same permissions. This is not antifragility. This is the illusionary privilege of comfortability.

You may immerse yourself in the work you want, and put in the lowest amount of effort to satisfice your work bar. That is also not antifragility. It just signifies that you are out of *frankenberries* to give. It's time to find more meaningful work.

Playing with something to lose is the exact opposite of the scenarios mentioned above. When you put something of your own on the line, not only do you buttress the concept of taking extreme ownership, but you also elicit your absolute best performance. If you bet with someone else's money, do you care about the outcomes as much as if you risk your own?

This mentality shows up all the time in people who flourish through living gamefully. I spent a summer recording an album in Jacksonville, FL in the early 2000s. After rehearsal or recording, my *barkada* (Tagalog for close neighborhood buddies) would inevitably meet to go bowling. This activity became very stale, very quickly. At two weeks, we were checking our flip phones, bored, and disengaged from the game and each other. While we could have raised the stakes monetarily, we did something better.

Before each round, a dance move was identified. If you rolled a gutter ball, you had to dance the move back to your seat of shame. Our game was rebranded as humili-bowling. Not only did it max out on the entertainment scale, but we were all consistently bowling the highest scores of our lives. The stakes weren't life or death, but the thought of having to do the worm back to our chairs, as the rest of the alley watched, was enough to focus and perform at the most critical time. Luckily, this works in almost any area— the higher stakes part, not the dancing part.

If you're a perfectionist, anything less than a stellar performance could cause hesitation, anxiety, or despair. Know that most situations are not do-or-die scenarios. It's only your gremlin turning on the spotlight effect to exaggerate your loss. When turmoil hits, don't disengage and blame. Respond as if you have something to lose.

Coupled with the growth mindset from extreme ownership, playing with something to lose will make you stronger during the most chaotic circumstances.

Class 28: Addition by Subtraction

"Delete."
—Matt Hardy

Delete behaviors that are anything less than helpful in your reaching your optimal state. Start with behaviors that are deleterious to your well-being and your business. This process is called *via negativa*. Instead of focusing on what you should do, concentrate on what not to do. By eliminating your harmful habits, you make yourself less open to vulnerability and risk. This brings you toward antifragility.

This should seem like an innocuous chapter as many people practice this ritual during their New Year's Resolution or Lent. Willpower and waypower are the strategies to follow through on when eliminating harmful vices.

Once you eliminate the bad habits, take *via negativa* to another level and eliminate neutral habits that have no positive or negative effect on your life to make room for good habits. Level up. Eliminate good habits to make room for great habits.

Here's what I want you to get out of this chapter. *Via negativa* doesn't just have an additive effect on your growth; it has an exponential effect like a good investment, and like kaizen. If you practice both *via negativa* and kaizen, prepare for explosive growth.

Start practicing *via negativa* now. What is the least beneficial habit, thought, or role that stands in the way of achieving your BHAG? Can you honestly eliminate it now? If not, what is a plan of action to delete it from your life?

Class 29: Make Every Micro-second Meaningful

"You take the good. You take the bad. You take them both and there you have the facts of life."
—Alan Thicke

There is the tendency to think that pain is the impetus for human development. In a deficit-based perspective, personal growth has the potential to be the result of traumatic events and tremendous losses. But what about a case where a person has ostensibly no major or identifiable trauma? Is it fair to say that a life devoid of trauma is a flourishing one? If you find yourself settling or striving, what is the activation energy that promotes ecstatic human growth?

Anne-Marie Roepke, Jane McGonigal, and a litany of researchers present wonderful ways to merge both growths as a result of trauma (Post-Traumatic Growth) or as a result of joy (Post-Ecstatic Growth). The thriver model links these two concepts by saying it's not about perceived trauma or joy, but more the saliency of the experience. In other words, value is derived from the meaning that a person gives to a particular experience.

Whatever you are doing this second has the same potential to create an "AHA" moment as powerfully growth-inducing as your worst trauma or greatest joy. And it entails a constant shift into the now. Staying in the present allows you to spot your muse instead of walking by it as you count red cars. The frenetic pace slows down and each moment becomes a perfect snapshot for you to derive inspiration. As you start to string together each micro-second, your life becomes fluid, animated, and incredibly purposeful.

There are an array of activities that can work for you. If you don't know where to begin, here are a few activities recommended by Jon Kabat-Zinn, author of the Mindfulness-Based Stress Reduction technique:

- Take a walk to gain perspective and awareness
- Turn daily tasks into mindful moments by merely paying attention to them
- Create
- Pay attention to your breathing
- Unitask (opposite of multitask)

- Know when NOT to check your phone
- Seek out new experiences
- Feel the feels by accepting your emotions, not reacting to them
- Meditate
- Be conscious of what you are putting in your body and mind
- Don't take yourself so seriously
- Give space for your mind to wander

Class 30: Create Infinite Pathways with Unlimited Opportunities

"Become a possibilitarian. No matter how dark things seem to be or actually are, raise your sights and see possibilities— always see them, for they're always there."
—**Norman Vincent Peale**

What do these things have in common: peanut butter and jelly, Hall and Oates, waypower and higher consciousness? They're all exponentially better together.

When waypower and higher consciousness are used in tandem, they create a type of antifragility where every action is the perfect move toward your goal.

Imagine your BHAG. Now imagine your primary strategy to attain your goal. This is one particular pathway to achieve that goal.

Now imagine moving along that pathway and coming across an unforeseen challenge. Being in a lower consciousness state will result in frustration or feeling as if the universe is conspiring against you. A higher consciousness state will feel more energized. Everything is happening as it should. Everything is an opportunity. So the higher your consciousness, the fewer challenges appear to be obstacles— and the more they become opportunities. Increase your higher consciousness through repurposing your gremlins and making every mini-second meaningful.

Think of a completely different strategy to get to your goal. This strategy is another pathway that you can take. It will come with a completely different set of challenges. Using the "if (obstacle), then I will (specific action)" MCII technique, you can identify the internal challenges.

As you visualize the BHAG associated with your extraordinary future, plan your journey on the second pathway. The more pathways you can imagine, the stronger your waypower becomes. The higher your waypower and higher consciousness, the more impossible it will be to *not* reach your BHAG.

Class 31: Simultaneously Take
the Road Most & Least Travelled

"Quantum theory dictates that a very tiny thing can absorb energy only in discrete amounts, can never sit perfectly still, and can literally be in two places at once."
—**Adrian Cho**

Identify your multiple pathways to achieve any particular goal. Use mental contrasting and implementation intentions (if…then I will…) to create a plan for your inner blocks. As much as you can pack your proverbial knapsack, your agency does have limitations. So outside of your agency is an external world that can get quite volatile and unpredictable. Instead of holding fast to one pathway, take multiple pathways with different strategies.

Start by looking at the safety, the return on investment, and the time to completion on each of your pathways. Optimally, find a pathway that's safe— with a high return— and with a short journey duration. Usually at least one of these three elements is not optimal. So you're more likely to identify pathways that are safe, have a high return, but the journey duration is very long. Or you might find a risky pathway that yields high return in a very short duration.

The former strategy is a hyper-conservative approach with almost no risk of ruin. Like a winding paved road, it will withstand during the most chaotic times. The latter strategy is a hyper-aggressive approach with high risk but a tremendous upside. So the first path provides robust support with the tradeoff of a long journey, while the second approach is a dilapidated bridge that can come apart with a sudden gust.

While you can take a more prudent approach to business, a prudent path is still only one path, and it too is vulnerable to chaos.

In both life and business, few rules say you must take one approach or the other. So don't limit yourself.

Use what is called the barbell strategy. On one end, deploy a hyper-conservative approach to hold your investment's safe and on the other, deploy the hyper-aggressive approach to open up leverage and speculation. Even in the most entropic situations, this is your best strategy for your business to be antifragile.

Look around, and you will see the barbell strategy being used everywhere. You see it in bond investment strategy. In roulette, you'll see an individual placing both high risk and low risk bets. Everton Football Club used the barbell strategy to perplex other teams and move them from the dregs of facing relegation to winning the Premiere League Championship the next year.

In your coaching business, you can use the barbell strategy to generate clients. The hyper-conservative approach could be organically growing your email list and feeding the group with content regularly, in hopes that they might purchase a cheaper introductory package one day with the possibility of offering a backend of more expensive 1-on-1 coaching. The hyper-aggressive approach would be to spend money on social media ads to sign up for webinars that lead to breakthrough sessions and offer high-end coaching clients.

In working with a limited budget, try hybridizing these two approaches using the barbell technique. Apply the Pareto Principle and start with a 20 percent hyper-aggressive strategy and an 80 percent hyper-conservative strategy, and then adjust the percentages based on return. Because of the volatility of social media and ad costs and policies, make sure you always have a more conservative approach to fall back on.

Chapter Eight
A FRAMEWORK TO DIE GAMEFULLY

"Something has to die for something new to live."
—Nadia Bolz-Weber

Birth. Growth. Maturation. Death. Renewal. The wheel keeps turning.

Have you ever bit into a slice of pizza so hot that there's a little piece of dead skin dangling from the roof of your mouth? In a matter of 24 hours, the cells are replaced. On the grandest of scales, this happens when stars explode in a glorious supernova only to collapse on themselves. This takes more than 24 hours.

And somewhere in the middle of this hullabaloo is you, an unapologetic coach, with a pocketful of fresh hopes and dreams. This section is not about the death of our physical bodies. It's about transformation in its truest sense. If you want to embrace your new life as a coach, it's time to part ways with the old.

Your current job is a burned piece of skin on the roof of your mouth. After it heals, you'll look back and see that it was a slight annoyance. It heals quicker than you think. While you are antifragile, take advantage of this time to add activation energy to your ecstatic growth. The wheel is coming back around. That feeling of inner turmoil will return and mix the perfect ingredients for another revolution. The birth of the unapologetic coach marks the death of the aspiring one.

It's like an etch-a-sketch for your soul. You create something special. A little shake-up. And you start anew with great memories of sketches past, and refined skills to improve your next masterpiece. The original framework stays intact but feels a little different. It's because you're different.

Let's revisit the gameful framework as it is expansive to accommodate your growth. First your obstacles do not go away. They magnify as you level-up. Now let's look at the other three principles in greater detail.

Class 32: Bigger Decisions

"Life is full of tough decisions, and nothing makes them easy. But the worst ones are really your personal koans, and tormenting ambivalence is just the sense of satori rising. Try, trust, try, and trust again, and eventually

you'll feel your mind change its focus to a new level of understanding."

—Martha Beck

Han Solo is my ideal client. Why? The dude's got mad flight skills and does it in a jalopy of a space craft. He's got bills to pay. He's a loner, but definitely doesn't need a motivational speaker. And when he's around the Princess, he's kind of vulnerable and goofy. When he stops undervaluing his strengths, he ultimately rises to the occasion.

What I love about Solo is that on the way to greatness, he almost backs out on his friends. He is an everyman caught up in something huge— he didn't sign up for this! Even a *bad dude* like Solo had to confront his fears. But something huge happened: He connected his capacity to act, his agency in the world to something larger than himself. His call was sudden, and he only answered by leading the Rebel Alliance.

As you come closer to your ideal self, you may find yourself resisting certain callings. Yet at some point, the ringing is so loud that you are volunteering for things for which you never thought you'd sign up. The choice for you to take a deep breath (or not) in Chapter Two was voluntary. You took agency over one breathe. When you connect your agency to the greater good, the game becomes epic (McGonigal, 2011), and your journey becomes heroic (Campbell, 2008).

For the same reason, the substitute teacher turned superhero from *Greatest American Hero* would be an ideal client. It wasn't his instruction-less space suit that made him a hero. It was that he answered a calling to serve something greater than himself despite the fact that the biggest advantage in his quest (the aforementioned indestructible alien spacesuit) was at-times utterly useless.

Class 33: More Gratifying Feedback Loops

"A master in the art of living draws no sharp distinction between his work and his play; his labor and his leisure; his mind and his body; his education and his recreation. He hardly knows which is which. He simply pursues his vision of excellence through whatever he is doing, and leaves others to determine whether he is working or playing. To himself, he always appears to be doing both."
—**Lawrence Pearsall Jacks**

Feedback loops don't only provide you with "cause and effect" for the choices you make as you live gamefully. As you become more aware of the feedback loops, you start looking forward to even the smallest energizer. As we come closer to living our ideal self, we start seeing the emergence of more energizers and fewer enervators. In his book *Energy Leadership*, Bruce

Schneider calls it anabolic and catabolic energy. Anabolic energy not only energizes but also promotes your growth, sense of well-being, and creativity. Catabolic energy wears you down, limits your options, and diminishes your sense of agency. If you, or your clients, have ever experienced a metaphorical "weight come off of your shoulders," that's a way to describe removing catabolic energy.

Use these feedback loops to savor your progress. If this were feedback loop 1.0, I would have asked you to be grateful for one thing a day as there are repeated clinical studies showing the health benefits of identifying things for which you are grateful.

The more aware of your feedback loop in your choice to pursue self-concordant goals, the more mental fireworks you'll experience. Savor each one. Since the brain is wired to find what you tell it to find, it will eventually find so many positive celebrations that you move far past identifying things for which to be grateful, you live gratefully. And to live in a state of gratuity is to live in abundance. In your service to others through coaching, your cup will runneth over. Make sure what spills over is shared with others.

Class 34: Deeper Objectives

"As you open yourself to living at your edge, your deepest purpose will slowly begin to make itself known. In

the meantime, you will experience layer after layer of purposes, each one getting closer and closer to the fullness of your deepest purpose. It is as if your deepest purpose is at the center of your being, and it is surrounded by concentric circles, each circle being a lesser purpose. Your life consists of penetrating each circle, from the outside toward the center."

—David Deida

As you complete your goals, new goals and objectives appear. Richer goals to complement your deeper purpose.

Do you remember your goals from ten years ago? Twenty years ago? Perhaps they were the same. Perhaps you've wanted to be a coach for twenty years? But how will your goals change when you attain becoming a successful coach?

As you pursue more sophisticated self-concordant goals, you'll find yourself experiencing, even more joy and richer fulfillment than ever. You're coming closer to your ideal self. And with it, the ability to communicate more articulately and with more clarity, your reason for getting out of bed on your worst day. I want you to revisit your answer to Chapter Two. Don't worry about it being specific and measurable; it's a meta-goal that goes after your purpose. The only thing I want you to review is if it answers the question "why" you exist. Mine hasn't changed very much in the past few years. It reads:

I want to empower as many people as possible while having as much fun as possible.

So I want you to answer this question again.

On your worst day, what gets you out of bed in the morning?

Write it down and keep it with you as you live gamefully 2.0. Revisit it when it's time to live gamefully 3.0.

Chapter Nine
GROWING PAINS

"Growth is painful. Change is painful. But, nothing is as painful as staying stuck where you do not belong."
—N. R. Narayana Murthy

A s discussed in the previous chapter, there is a catabolic aspect to advancement. The act of lifting weights has you repeating an exercise until you reach failure. The resulting micro-tears in the muscle fibers allow the body to rebuild stronger muscles that have adapted to the more substantial weight. After the catabolic damage, there is the inventible repair and generation of stronger and faster tissue. Science is magic.

At some points in your coaching journey, rest and nourishment will be vital to growth. Long-term strain leads to burnout without the right feedback loops for you to savor and celebrate regularly. This chapter examines the most common challenges that you may face in your development as a coach and entrepreneur.

Class 35: Rules Create Freedom

"I did it my way."
—**Frank Sinatra**

Rules create freedom. I'm not talking about rules and freedom from the lens of societal oppression. I'm talking about them from the standpoint of the freedom you want from a successful coaching business.

So the first freedom you have is to use game theory or not to craft your vocation. Create rules that promote flow and allow your willpower and waypower to flourish. How many hours of deep work are you committed to each week? What are the times you clock in and clock out? If there is an open-time slot, what are the other pathways with unlimited opportunities to walk down?

I also envision my absolute minimum annual salary. Divide it by 12 to get an approximate salary. Divide by four to get a weekly check. Divide by the number of deep work hours I put in a week. And there's the opportunity cost of my taking an hour off.

So as an example:

If you want to make, $120,000 a year in coaching, you'll make $10,000 a month ($120,000/12). This gives you $2,500 per week ($10,000/4). Assuming that you choose a 40-hour week, divide $2,500 by 40 hours. This gives you, $62.50 per hour. So imagine that every hour you skip, will cost you $62.50.

It may be an introvert thing, but my peak hours seem to coincide with the world being asleep. So marketing, writing copy, automation, this all can happen during the witching hours. This gives me huge blocks in the morning to exercise, spend time with family, and listen to Stern. Come 11 a.m. it's client acquisition and coaching time. Weekends are absolutely off-limits. So every day affords me micro-celebrations, every weekend is a meso-celebration, and I have time to plan for larger trips like my upcoming roller derby trip to Barcelona (macro-celebration).

It's not sexy, Tim Ferris-stuff. Nor is it a 7-figure, passive income strategy. It's an understanding that on the lowest level, I have a few hundred bucks to lose for taking an hour off. It's my stake in the game. And on the high level, I'm missing out on an ideal, high-end client who could refer me to more ideal, high-end clients.

Decide your rules, and hold yourself accountable to them until you outgrow your goals. That is the privilege of being an entrepreneur. And also enjoy the freedoms that come from your deep work— the daily, weekly, and dream celebrations.

Class 36: False Feedback

"I don't want your life!"
—James Van Der Beek

In my introduction to feedback loops in Chapter Two, I talked about how identifying and installing your feedback loop can be a game in itself. Problems occur when you identify performance and progress indicators that are not lined up with your personal values. You spend a reasonable amount of time figuring it out, while everyone else seemingly has their stuff figured out. From a very young age, you consciously and unconsciously pick up societal standards for success. Sometimes you might install some feedback loops that are completely incongruous with the game. This is what we call false feedback. This is any feedback that takes us further away from our ideal selves.

Money, prestige, influence— none of these are bad things. But when you're making a lot more money, and you aren't any more fulfilled, it's time to check the reliability and validity of your feedback loop. What sometimes happens in cases like this is that the pendulum swings in the opposite direction. Consequently, you face the possibility of replacing the emptiness of the first feedback loop with more hedonic, fast-acting pleasures— the sex, the drugs, the rock n' roll. And you're still left saying, "There's got to be more to life than this."

I knew that I was ready to coach when I was working in the University, and a 20-year alumni told me about how he had "everything he ever wanted in life." He made every grade, graduated at the top of his MBA class, made 7-figures on Wall Street, but every night he was blowing his earnings away on cocaine and hookers. He was acting on false feedback. Were there some past issues there? Probably. Could he use some treatment and therapy? Yes. Could he work with someone who could create space for him to develop an authentic, personally meaningful feedback loop? Definitely.

Class 37: Strengths Overuse

"A person's strength was always his weakness, and vice versa."
—**Viet Thanh Nguyen**

Once you find a strength that works in a few domains, you may want to try your strength out in other contexts. In fact, I have a coaching colleague who is making 6-figures as an administrator, but struggles with coaching because her strengths of directing others do not translate well in coaching. While it is important to use our strengths in a new way, using them in the wrong context can actually have a detrimental effect. Not only is the person less successful in achieving their goals, but research testifies of lower flourishing and life satisfaction, higher depression, and negative impacts on relationships and life in those who overuse their strengths.

Class 38: Gremlins Two

"First she said we were to keep clear of the Sirens, who sit and sing most beautifully in a field of flowers; but she said I might hear them myself so long as no one else did. Therefore, take me and bind me to the crosspiece half way up the mast; bind me as I stand upright, with a bond so fast that I cannot possibly break away, and lash the rope's ends to the mast itself. If I beg and pray you to set me free, then bind me more tightly still."

—**Homer**, *The Odyssey*

Your gremlin is in your mind. So it can use any practical or intellectual wisdom that you have acquired against you. As you grow, so does your gremlin. If you've followed the steps in the book, you successfully created a clear purpose statement tied to serving the greater good. You have a multi-year vision that has been chunked down into goals. And if you're already practicing kaizen and building your antifragility, your moxie is looking pretty dope.

At the most inopportune time, the gremlins will show up bigger, badder, stronger, and faster. It is a good sign as, consciously or not, you will recognize that something big is about to tip in your life. Perhaps you've been hustling for months to give a killer speech to your ideal clients and ten minutes before you go on stage, you feel your chest tighten. Or maybe it's a week before your manuscript is due and out of nowhere you freak out about how you're a total imposter. It's the well-meaning gremlin trying to protect you with antiquated malarkey.

Now here's the coolest part. Your gremlin won't return alone. It returns with Sirens with tactics used to lead you astray. Sirens give completely new goals to shift your priorities away from your ideal self. They pull at your heartstrings and seduce. They seem ridiculously real and pull you in a completely different direction than your goals.

I am not without my Sirens, and my editor called me out on it once I got my book topic approved. She warned me that, along the way, I'll want to write a new book, have an emergency or shiny-new people will show up in my life. She was talking about the Sirens that would prevent me from finishing the project. I had a hurricane knock out my power for four days while writing this book. What my editor meant was that very real events could create fake distractions to not finish a book that could empower many people. Instead I wrote the antifragility chapter on a legal pad with a pen. First-world problems folks.

You have all the tools to thrive. Don't let a distraction completely topple it over. Get an experienced coach who will call you out on your Sirens.

Class 39: When Moxie Becomes Egotism

"We're so wrapped up with egotistical things, career, family, having enough money, meeting the mortgage, getting a new car, fixing the radiator when it breaks—we're involved in trillions of little acts just to keep going. So we don't get into the habit of standing back and looking at our lives and saying, Is this all? Is this all I want? Is something missing?"

—**Mitch Albom**

If you are taking theory to practice, sustained action alone will raise your self-confidence, your agency, your moxie. We already talked about how the external world may not take it well when individuals see you flourishing, but there's also an internal change that's both subtle but important to your long term happiness. To be fully masterful, you must embrace ego, the confidence you have in yourself. Your self-fulfillment will come in the form of your service to the greater good.

Egotism, however, comes when you feign service to the greater good in order to serve yourself usually from your inadequate moxie. Service to others is not actually your agenda. There is no reciprocity in your relationships because you're more interested in being correct than working with others. You pretend to be a virtuous friend, when you are looking for self-serving utility.

When this happens the unapologetic coach becomes the egotistical coach. Growth is always an option, but it won't happen in egotism. The game is over, for now (Alinsky, 1971).

Class 40: Outgrowing Your Tribe

"The higher you ascend, the smaller you appear to the eye of envy. But most of all they hate those who fly."
—**Friedrich Nietzsche**

Here come the heavy social ramifications for voluntarily going after your own vocation. The settler tells you that you're making things way too hard on yourself. The striver tells you that you are a joke. They all play by conventions. Who are you to think you're above those conventions— you've become the rebel, maverick, iconoclast. New people want to collaborate, and you're not quite sure what their intentions are. This is where the solitude of the hero's journey blurs with the confusion of loneliness.

This is the tough part again: individuals can choose to see you as an ingenious, efficient solution, or a cheap, disposable novelty. Equipped with the knowledge of Aristotle's useful and hedonic friendships, you know that you have ceased to be of use or bring pleasure to someone else. But it's never easy.

It's why you probably hid your wings in the first place.

Steven Pressfield says, "When we see others beginning to live their authentic lives, it drives us crazy if we have not lived out our own." And this is the number one conversation I have with clients who are considering becoming a coach and those who are over twenty years in the game.

This shows up in multiple ways. I have one client, Owen, who openly admits that he is fueled by the catabolic energy to prove his former colleagues wrong. Not a super great long-term strategy, but it beats a motivational speech any day. Another client, Autumn, has serious trepidation about losing all of her friends, because they already "tease her" about making them feel bad with her ostensibly perfect life. Yet the same client knows she's feeling envious of others who are living out there dream.

Owen and Autumn are ascending into their ideal selves and dealing with the natural growing pains of leaving their former selves behind. They know, in different ways, what's not sustainable. And know that there will be new utilitarian, hedonic, and virtuous relationships at this new altitude.

Chapter Ten
CONCLUSION

"Witnessing and interacting with excellent individuals can create opportunities for enrichment of the self and society. Inspiring leaders, caring benefactors, and selfless saints do more than draw praise from emotionally-responsive witnesses; these exemplary others inspire people to improve themselves, their behavior, and their relationships. Elevation, gratitude, and admiration are not just flavors of happiness. They are a part of the human emotional repertoire that, until now has been largely unexplored, and whose potential remains largely untapped."

—Jonathan Haidt

The Death of an Aspiring Coach

Earlier this year, I was booked to speak at an event for solopreneurs on the benefits of positive psychology and self-coaching principles in business application. My parents were in town and went to the venue with me. I bet they thought I was going to give a motivational speech. As the lecture room filled with no one, every gremlin of doubt and insecurity surfaced. And by the time I took the stage, I found myself staring into an audience of my parents, my son, my cousins, and five strangers.

Epic fail from the start. I felt pitiful and shameful. It was like the audience was embarrassed for me.

The gremlins were having a field day, while I was surrounded by the most inner circle of my tribe, holding notes prepared for a large audience. I did the only thing I knew I could. I took in a deep breath and had one of those collywobble exhales, where you literally feel the butterflies moving around in your stomach.

: I gave my presentation points, recognized that this was the most unique audience I ever had the privilege of presenting to, and asked each audience member what they wanted to get most from my presentation. From there, the audience took the lead. Strangers became friends. A hostile environment became welcoming. We were all playing the game— as a tribe. It was a moment of total synchronicity and flow.

Afterward, one of the tribe members approached my parents and said, "Your son is really special. You must be proud." They were proud, and it was cool to see. Dweck (1997) says that my mindset was fixed because their approval felt so darn gratifying. As much as I studied positive psychology, coaching, and resilience, this is what finding opportunity in the midst of a dire situation looks like— and more importantly, *feels* like. As someone who had been reconciling valuing both collectivism and individualism, I always felt like I needed to explain *who I am* and *what I do*. Sometimes your tribe just needs to see how hard you work to balance the art and science of living gamefully for themselves. It doesn't come around often. But it happened in this instance. Within two hours, the feedback loop came full circle in the most frustrating and gratifying of ways. It indicated the end of a successful journey and the start of a new one.

That was the day my life as an aspiring coach ended, and a new one— as an unapologetic coach began.

My Wish for You

There are over seven billion people in this world. Aside from a few sociopaths, I haven't met one person who hasn't felt suffering or pain. If you are called to serve through coaching, enough people will benefit from your stepping into your more ideal self. My wish for you is that you distinguish between your calling and the idea of a calling, make a decision to act, and know that the members of your tribe, the few virtuous ones, may never be able to articulate what you do— but your growth will ultimately inspire them to be their more ideal selves.

The structure for living gamefully is a blank canvas for you to paint. It's the stage for you to improvise, and the platform upon which you shout your epic purpose.

Owning your strengths and repurposing your gremlins provide you with a larger pallet of colors. Exciting your tribe gives you reciprocity to identify people who are hungry for your service and those who hunger to nourish you. Visioning a realistic but amazing future creates the hope, willpower, and waypower for you to pursue goals. But chunking down your vision to action steps will give you the moxie to coach unapologetically.

With the upswing of your moxie, move beyond resilience to antifragility. And you'll find yourself on another level. Keep playing the game, knowing that it gets more challenging as your purpose refines, flow becomes something you can evoke, your agency grows, and you fall into living in complete awe and gratitude. Remember that your growth is not linear, and it may feel as if every time you progress, you digress. But you are also growing upward.

Creating hospitable places for strangers is a major thematic point in this book and in your efficacy as a coach. Don't forget to include your ideal self. The familiarity you gain with your ideal self is the self-actualization. It opens the door to self-transcendence. This is when your ideal self becomes a servant to something much greater.

Praxis is the process through which you take theory to practice. My intention is that you embody these concepts presented in this book via praxis and fully utilize every ounce of yourself to serve, live, love, and play.

As you continue this journey, your moxie will rise so much that it will be hard to believe what you perceived were once insurmountable odds when you first started the journey as an emergent coach. As you rise above the dark clouds of despair and indifference, the critiques of others won't even consume a nanosecond of your attention.

This is where I am most excited for you. Because others will take notice of your stability, trustworthiness, compassion, and hope. Day after day of pounding the rock through committed and sustained action demonstrates your stability. Being open about the nature of relationships and creating a sense of community for your tribe builds your trustworthiness. Others will notice your compassion as you practice deep love and feeding your tribe. The combination of vision, willpower, and waypower are the ingredients for one of the most powerful indicators of success— hope. This is the way of the unapologetic coach. More than any masters-level coaching certification or sales funnel, this is what will draw people to you, earn the deference of your virtuous friends, and inspire the masses.

And I guess, if you need any motivation, for your sake, for my sake, for goodness sake: Wake up. Get out of bed.

> *"Be water, my friend."*
> —**Bruce Lee**

REFERENCES

Alinsky, S. (1971). Rules for radicals: A pragmatic primer for realistic radicals. New York: Random House.

Aristotle, Ross, W. D., & Brown, L. (2009). *The Nicomachean ethics*. Oxford: Oxford University Press.

Bandura, A. (1997). *Self-efficacy: The exercise of control*. New York: W.H. Freeman.

Ben-Shahar, T. (2017). Positive Psychology 103: Realizing dreams, Lecture 3: Self-concordant goals. Retrieved from https://wholebeinginstitute.com.

Benson, H., & Proctor, W. (2011). *Relaxation revolution: The science and genetics of mind body healing*. New York: Scribner.

Campbell, J. (2008). *The hero with a thousand faces*. Novato, CA: New World Library.

Dierolf, K., Meier, D. & Szabo, P. (2009*). Coaching Plain & Simple: Solution-focused brief coaching essentials.* New York: W.W. Norton & Co.

Dweck, C. S. (2016). *Mindset: The new psychology of success.* New York: Ballentine Books.

Fredrickson, B. L. (2013). *Love 2.0: How our supreme emotion affects everything we feel, think, do, and become.* New York: Hudson Street Press.

Hyde, L. (2017). *Trickster makes this world: How disruptive imagination creates culture.* Edinburgh: Canongate Books.

McGonigal, J. (2011). *Reality is broken: Why games make us better and how they can change the world.* New York: Penguin Publishing Group.

McGonigal, J. (2016). *SuperBetter: The power of living gamefully.* Toronto: Penguin.

McMillan, D.W., & Chavis, D.M. (1986). Sense of community: A definition and theory. *Journal of Community Psychology*, 14(1), 6-23.

Nassim Nicholas Taleb (2012). *Antifragile: Things that gain from disorder.* New York: Random House.

Newport, C. (2018). *Deep work: Rules for focused success in a distracted world.* New York: Grand Central.

Oettingen, G., & Gollwitzer, P. M. (2010). Strategies of setting and implementing goals. In J. E. Maddux & J. P.

Tangney (Eds.), *Social psychological foundations of clinical psychology*. New York: The Guilford Press.

Niemiec, R. M. (2017). *Character strengths interventions*. Boston: Hogrefe Publishing.

Robbins, M. (2017). The 5 second rule: transform your life, work, and confidence with everyday courage. United States: Savio Republic.

Ryan, R. M., & Deci, E. L. (2000). Self-determination theory and the facilitation of intrinsic motivation, social development, and well-being. *American Psychologist*, 55(1), 68-78.

Schneider, B. D. (2010). *Energy leadership: Transforming your workplace and your life from the core*. Hoboken: John Wiley & Sons, Inc.

Sheldon, K. M., & Elliot, A. J. (1999). Goal striving, need satisfaction, and longitudinal well-being: The self-concordance model. *Journal of Personality and Social Psychology*, 76(3), 482-497.

Spence, G. B. & Oades, L. G. (2011). Coaching with self-determination theory in mind: Using theory to advance evidence-based coaching practice. *International Journal of Evidence-Based Coaching and Mentoring*, 9 (2), 37-55.

Ware, B. (2013). *The top five regrets of the dying: A life transformed by the dearly departing*. Carlsbad, CA: Hay House.

Wrzesniewski, A., McCauley, C. R., Rozin, P., & Schwartz, B. (1997). Jobs, careers, and callings: People's relations to their work. *Journal of Research in Personality*, 31, 21-33.

ACKNOWLEDGMENTS

Writing is hard.

Boyd White. You were the first person who told me to ditch premed and to continue writing without boundaries during my first year of college. I still remember your making me read my paper about Bruce Lee, wisdom teeth and Tori Amos.

Thank you to the faculty of the University of Georgia's College Student Affairs and Administration Doctoral Program for giving me writing boundaries. Years of APA formats and human development theory did not fall on deaf ears.

To the students, staff, and faculty of Emory University, I was given the sunlight, water and swords to be born a million times over— a million and one thank you's.

To the Wholebeing Institute Certificate in Positive Psychology and team AHA Shhhh. I respectfully submit the second draft of my final project! Mic drop.

Annaliza Thomas Toussaint. These were our musings roomie. Thank you.

Thank you to Institute for Professional Excellence in Coaching (iPEC) for giving me the space to release my catabolic energy over and over.

Angela Lauria and the Author Incubator family. Thank you for driving home what Boyd couldn't get through a few years ago. Huzzah!

Hilary Booker. You could accelerate this process and make me antifragile. Thank you.

Thank you to Russ Rufino and the Clients on Demand family for being the last piece to the coaching puzzle.

To the Metro-Atlanta Roller Derby community, thanks for showing me and Manila Ice that there are always things way harder than writing. Harumph.

To team titofelix/Tsinilas, who gave me a "penny for my thoughts" on how to live with the volume at 11, and how to get it all done before Wrestlemania.

To the Greater Good Strategic & Life Coaching community, see you this Friday.

To the Morgan James Publishing team: Special thanks to David Hancock, CEO & Founder for believing in me and my message. To my Author Relations Manager, Margo Toulouse, thanks for making the process seamless and easy. Many more thanks to everyone else, but especially Jim Howard, Bethany Marshall, and Nickcole Watkins.

And, to the Cordons, Anoos, Dizons, Reddys, and my extended familia—maraming salamat po!!

Special Thanks to the Book Launch Team
Alison Proffit
Annaliza Thomas Toussaint
April Steele
Bel Ora-a
Belen Loreto Grand
Billie Jo Bauman
Callie Cummings
Celeste Waid
Christina Dela Cruz
Hilary Booker
Joel Yuzon Ignacio
Joumay Fiel
Lexi Mitchell
Lynn Wasylyk Bagdasian
Marco Balducci
Marsha Vaughn
Melissa Morrison
Michelle Plavnik

Michelle Wartgow
Nathan Adlam
Nikki Tobias
Rachel Booth
Ricky Boggs
Sergio Livingston
Sheree Williams Gibson
Stacey Agbonzé
Steven Trash Logan
Traci Paz Hudgin
Varick Rosete

ABOUT THE AUTHOR

 Marc Cordon, MPH, ACC is the founder of Greater Good Strategic & Life Coaching which serves rebellious entrepreneurs, misfit coaches, and ostensible iconoclasts who are committed to changing history for the better. For over two decades, he has assisted countless people in self-development through speaking engagements, retreats, mini-courses, and 1-on-1 advising and mentoring. Marc loves spending time with his family and plays roller derby under the nickname of Manila Ice.

Website: www.iambeyondresilient.com
Facebook: www.facebook.com/groups/beyondresilent
Email: marc@marccordon.com

THANK YOU

I hope the ideas in this book provided the activation energy for you to take your personal life and your coaching to the next level. Keep in touch as you live gamefully. Celebrate your wins with me. And let me know how I can assist you.

Even if you took action on a handful of classes in this book, you have created momentum for yourself. Keep going!

To assist you on your journey to become beyond resilient and experience extraordinary growth, I have recorded a 4-part mini-course. Use the mini-course to craft your dream coaching business. Get it now at www.iambeyondresilient.com.

God speed. Good luck. And I'll talk to you soon.

Marc

Morgan James
Speakers Group

www.TheMorganJamesSpeakersGroup.com

We connect Morgan James published
authors with live and online events
and audiences who will benefit
from their expertise.